The Urgency of Marxist-Christian Dialogue

the URGENCY of MARXIST-CHRISTIAN DIALOGUE

Herbert L Aptheker

1817

HARPER & ROW, PUBLISHERS
NEW YORK, EVANSTON, AND LONDON

FIRST EDITION

LIBRARY OF CONGRESS CATALOG CARD NUMBER: 73-109081

To the new Joshua, with love and hope

Contents

The Urgency of Marxist-Christian Dialogue

Chapter One

Views and Problems:
An Introduction

1

What conception of religion does one find in the philosophies of
Karl Marx and Friedrich Engels?

Marxism sees the source, the root of religious feeling in a sense
of awe and wonder and of helplessness and misery. In the earliest
stages of history, religious feeling stemmed from man's inability to
comprehend and therefore to deal effectively with the forces of
nature. With the development of social and economic classes, an
additional fount existed in the form of the oppression endured by
the producing masses and their inability to comprehend the reasons
for this oppression and hence to overcome it. To the degree that the
conquest of nature has been partial and the unlocking of its mysteries far from complete, both these founts have operated in class
societies to swell the ocean of religious feeling.

Marxism sees the source of major religious institutions in class
divisions and the consequent division of labor, in the appearance
of state power, and in the usefulness of those religious institutions
for the maintenance of that power. Since classes are not only different but also often antagonistic, dissident religious institutions do

appear that challenge, more or less severely, the status quo. They face persecution, and survival is achieved at the cost of some degree of acquiescence.

The clearest and briefest Marxist definition of religion is in Engels' *Anti-Dühring* (1878): "... the fantastic reflection in men's minds of those external forces which control their daily life, a reflection in which the terrestrial forces assume the form of supernatural forces."[1] To the extent that religion is this "fantastic reflection"—distorted, springing from and reflecting alienation—and to the extent that religion holds to the supernatural (the antiscientific), Marxism is radically opposed to religion.

Marxism treats religion historically as it does and must treat everything, since the dialectical quality of Marxism sees all phenomena in a dynamic, rather than a static manner, and sees process as the essence of all reality. Thus, most particularly concerning Christianity, Marxism stresses the significant contrast between early and late Christianity. It is appropriate to illustrate this fact from some classical Marxist writings. Friedrich Engels, in an essay "On the History of Early Christianity," published in the last year of his life (1895), wrote:

The history of early Christianity has notable points of resemblance with the modern working-class movement. Like the latter, Christianity was originally a movement of oppressed people: it first appeared as the religion of slaves and emancipated slaves, of poor people deprived of all rights, of peoples subjugated or dispersed by Rome. Both Christianity and the workers' socialism preach forthcoming salvation from bondage and misery; Christianity places this in a world beyond, after death, in heaven; socialism places it in this world, in a transformation of society. Both are persecuted and baited, their adherents are despised and made the objects of exclusive laws, the former as enemies of the human race, the latter as enemies of the state, the enemies of religion, the family, [the] social order. And in spite of all persecution, nay, even spurred on by it, they forge victoriously, irresistibly ahead. Three hundred years after its appearance Christianity was the recognized state religion in the Roman World Empire, and in barely sixty years socialism has won itself a position which makes its victory absolutely certain.

2

THE URGENCY OF MARXIST-CHRISTIAN DIALOGUE

In the same essay Engels declares of the early Christian writings: ". . . they could just as well have been written by one of the prophetically minded enthusiasts of the [First] International." In an earlier essay, "Bauer and Early Christianity" (1882), Engels had written that "the essential feature" of "the new religious philosophy"—he meant Christianity—was that it "reverses the previous world order, seeks its disciples among the poor, the miserable, the slaves and the rejected, and despises the rich, the powerful and the privileged. . . ."

The historical, developmental treatment of religion that is basic to the Marxist approach is spelled out with particular clarity in *Anti-Dühring*. Three paragraphs will illustrate this:

> In Catholicism there was first the *negative equality of all human beings before God as sinners* [Engels' italics], and, more narrowly construed, the equality of all children of God redeemed by the grace and the blood of Christ. Both versions are grounded on the role of Christianity as the religion of slaves, the banished, the dispossessed, the persecuted, the oppressed. With the victory of Christianity this circumstance was relegated to the rear and prime importance attached next to the antithesis between believers and pagans, orthodox and heretics.

> With the rise of the cities and thereby of the more or less developed elements of the bourgeoisie, as well as of the proletariat, the demand for equality as a condition of bourgeois existence was bound gradually to resurge, interlinked with the proletariat's drawing the conclusion to proceed from political to social equality. This naturally assumed a religious form, sharply expressed for the first time in the Peasant War.

> The bourgeois side was first formulated by Rousseau, in trenchant terms but still on behalf of all humanity. As was the case with all the demands of the bourgeoisie, so here too the proletariat cast a fateful shadow beside it and drew its own conclusions (Babeuf).

One should take account of Engels' point that while institutionalized religion generally seeks to bulwark the status quo, the content of the religious affirmations—whose sources are not unitary—has its own logic, and may appeal to and does appeal to different classes. That is, while ruling classes may wish to employ religious feeling and belief as forces for the retention of their power, nevertheless religion, being a mass phenomenon that transcends classes,

3

may serve as the justification for and inspiration of vast popular movements, including movements that are revolutionary.

Marxism, then, emphasizes the revolutionary quality of early Christianity. Marx himself, as a youngster in the *gymnasium*, wrote a paper entitled "Observations of a Young Man on the Choice of a Life-Work," in which he manifested his admiration for the Christ figure and in which he declared: "To men God gave a universal aim —to ennoble mankind and oneself." This is, certainly, the "pre-Marxist" Marx, but the reverence is to be noted and the particular point that attracted Marx to Christ is significant. This idea recurs in the later writing of the fully mature Marx, writing, for example, in 1855 on an antichurch demonstration in London, he excoriated the established church for its callousness and reactionary policy and went on to contrast it with the teaching of Jesus. Marx added: "The classical saint of Christianity mortified *his* body for the salvation of the souls of the masses; the modern, educated saint mortifies the *bodies of the masses* for the salvation of his own soul."

Marxism repeatedly notes the connection between religiosity and rebellion, but it is a religiosity of masses who see in their religious beliefs goads not for pie in the sky but for battle on earth. Engels wrote of such mass religiosity in Europe prior to the French Revolution in *Feuerbach and the End of Classical German Philosophy* (1886): "The sentiments of the masses were fed with religion to the exclusion of all else; it was therefore necessary to put forward their own interests in a religious guise in order to produce an impetuous movement." The whole of Engels' book, *The Peasant War in Germany* (1850), spells this out.

It is sometimes held that Marxism sees the connection between religion and rebelliousness as hypocritical or demagogic. That is, I think, an error. Marxism frequently sees religion as a subjective form for the expression of objective content, but this is analytical and in no way invidious. Questions of motivation are not, or need not be, involved. There are no better illustrations of this than those that saturate American history. For example, no Marxist would deny either the revolutionary passion or the religious inspiration of John Brown. The motto of Thomas Jefferson was "Resistance to Tyranny is Obedience to God"; and while Jefferson's religion was

4

not denominational, there is no doubt as to his fundamental religiosity. American slavemasters taught their chattel only one lesson in religious instruction (attendance at which was often compulsory): be meek and docile, accept your hard lot on this earth as the portion of an omnipotent God, know that the hardness of the lot is a measure of His love for you, and understand, therefore, that to protest against your position in life would be blasphemy. Many slaves rejected this teaching, but they did not reject religion. On the contrary, their religion was the religion of early Christianity because, like those who created that Christianity, they, too, were slaves and among the wretched of the earth. The slave-rebellion leaders were all religious men. Nat Turner preached to his comrades that the first shall be last and the last first; that God so hated slaveowners He sent fearful scourges among them; that He so loved slaves He parted the seas so they might escape bondage, and then brought the waters together again to drown the masters' pursuing armies. What was true of past popular struggles in the United States is also true in the present, as the mention of Martin Luther King, Jr., and A. J. Muste makes clear. How multifarious is religion is shown by the fact that Count Metternich and John Brown were contemporaries and brothers in Christ!

The classical statement of Marxism on religion, at least the most often quoted or excerpted statement, is, of course, the "opium" one. It is true that Americans are in a great hurry—going nowhere, Brecht commented—still everyone should read the essay in which the phrase appears; if one does not have time to read the whole essay, which is not long, one must make time to read the two paragraphs in which the "opium" appears. Here they are, from Marx's essay, "Contribution to the Critique of Hegel's Philosophy of Right" (1844):

> Religious distress is at the same time the *expression* of real distress and the *protest* against real distress. Religion is the sigh of the oppressed creature, the heart of a heartless world, just as it is the spirit of a spiritless situation. It is the *opium* of the people.[2]
>
> The abolition of religion as the *illusory* happiness of the people is required for their real happiness. The demand to give up the illusions about its condition is the *demand to give up a condition which needs illusions.*

The criticism of religion is therefore *in embryo the criticism of the vale of woe*, the *halo* of which is religion. [Marx's italics.]

Dismissing this passage as some sort of vulgar atheism or as a cranky and mechanical rejection of religion per se, or even as an attack upon religion, constitutes a complete distortion. It is as though one quoted Christ as saying, "Go and sin." He did say that, of course, but if one wishes to convey his thought one should complete the sentence: "Go and sin no more."

Marx, in the two paragraphs quoted, is emphasizing the protest potential of religion; he also stresses its beauty and its nature as a source of refreshment. Central to his thought is the insistence that religion is a necessity, given the existence of oppressive, unjust, or unreasonable relationships. Marx insisted upon the deeply persistent quality of religion because it serves real needs. In his great work *Capital,* which presumably reflects the fully mature Marx, he wrote: "The religious reflex of the real world can, in any case, only finally vanish, *when the practical relations of every-day life offer to man none but perfectly intelligible and reasonable relations with regard to his fellowmen and to nature"* (italics added). On religion, despite frequent charges to this effect, Marxism does not err in underestimating the lasting potential; in other areas Marxism does, I think, err in this direction, notably in terms of nationalism.

Let it be added that while Marxism may be absolved of this error, not all who consider themselves Marxists are innocent. Some Christians have been frank in noting the aberrations and failures of Christianity; they insist upon distinguishing between Christianity and Christians, and such distinctions are valid. The same sense of reality, not to speak of compassion, is often absent when Christians (and others) consider the differences, or even contradictions, that appear between Marxism and the actual behavior, at times, of Marxists.

Marxism, manifesting a profound humanism as the heart of its inspiration, naturally opposes religious persecution. It opposes coercive methods aimed at religion. This was, incidentally, one of the many points of conflict between Marxism and anarchism, or at least of some aspects of anarchism (between, for instance, Marx and

Blanqui). In its attitude toward religion, one may illustrate the fact that Marxism was created not only in combat with the capitalism of the Right but also with the anarchism, Blanquism and terrorism of the ultra-Left. The attack upon religious persecution recurs in the classical writings.

At the same time, Marxism always advocates a secular society, favoring separation of church and state. In so doing, it makes clear that it demands more than religious toleration, for that would be intolerant towards antireligion. In his *Critique of the Gotha Program* (1875), Marx made explicit that he favored the toleration of agnosticism and atheism, as well as of all religions.

Marxism opposes professional atheists; it also opposes those whom Georg Lukacs once called religious atheists. That is, it opposes those who so vehemently and insistently attack God as to lead to the belief that they do protest too much. When individuals have reached positions wherein God is altogether unnecessary, and when the social order reaches the stage where religious concepts will no longer be necessary, religion will evaporate if Marxism is correct.

Marxists will argue their historical materialist position, of course, and will seek through their work and writings to show its validity, and socialist states will seek to educate their populations in a historical materialist direction. Marxism certainly is not indifferent, philosophically, to religion (any more than the reverse is true). But Marxism does see the multifarious sources of religion; it does distinguish between religious feeling and religious institution; it knows and insists that religious feelings often have impelled (and today still may impel) magnificent and effective progressive and revolutionary activity; that religious feeling means one thing to one class and another to another class; and that Marxism is itself a phenomenon in process. An attitude of contempt for religion is an anti-Marxist attitude; an attitude of superiority towards religious people is both anti-Marxist and contemptible.[3]

There have been such attitudes in the past among some Marxists. There have also been sectarian patterns of behavior in the past— and perhaps not only in the past—that to recall makes one's flesh crawl. Some of this has its roots in ignorance, in psychological failings, in reaction to persecution, and in the strain of the struggle. Much of it has its roots in the actual practices of established religion, which often induce a hostility that does not differentiate between the institution and the faith, between the practice and the idea, or, at least, aspects of the idea.

A fairly typical expression of the latter kind of opinion comes from James H. Maurer, a machinist, a member of the Pennsylvania legislature and of the Reading (Pa.) City Council, the President of the Pennsylvania Federation of Labor, and a vice-presidential candidate of the Socialist party, and is dated 1929:

> To hear preachers lament and rave about how so very, very long ago Joseph was sold into slavery for twenty pieces of silver can hardly be expected to arouse interest in the minds of people who know that the church not so many years ago not only condoned but actually defended chattel slavery. To go to a church and listen to a sermon about the sublimeness of being humble and meek, that no matter how desperate the struggle to live may be one should be contented and not envy the more fortunate, because God in His infinite wisdom has ordained that there shall be rich and poor, and that no matter how heavy one's burdens on this earth one should bear them meekly and look for reward in the world to come and remember that God loves the poor—such sermons naturally sound pleasing to the ears of the wealthy listeners, and the usual reward is a shower of gold and hearty congratulations by the sleek and well-fed members of the congregation. But to an intelligent worker such sermons sound like capitalistic propaganda, upon which he is constantly being fed up by every labor-exploiting concern in the country, and quite naturally he tries to avoid getting an extra dose of the same kind of buncombe on Sunday.[4]

Recently the Roman Catholic Church itself officially admitted the truth of this labor leader's indictment in the Pastoral Constitution on the Church in the Modern World, dated December 7, 1965, from Vatican II. The admission is stated with predictable delicacy and confined to footnotes. Footnote 130 reads:

> Whatever the regrettable misunderstandings that turned the "rights of man" into a rallying cry of the Church's bitter foes in the 18th and 19th centuries and entrenched the Church in a role of intransigent resistance to movements for social revolution in many parts of the world, the Council now makes it unequivocally plain that the Church intends to play its true

historic role as a champion of human rights and to align itself with those who fight for these rights.

Further along in the same document where the Church affirms its preference for political communities that "afford all their citizens the chance to participate freely and actively in establishing the constitutional bases," footnote 239 declares that the Church does not here mean to discriminate among political forms, but that:

> This passage stresses, however, the full compatibility of maximal representative government with the dignity of the human person. Here is clearly an advance from the suspicion of democracy that found favor in so many areas of Catholic thought throughout the nineteenth and into the present century.[5]

Religious anti-Marxism has some of its roots in literal and non-historic readings of certain writings by Marx and Lenin. Understandable possibilities of misreading occasionally do appear. Thus, one may read in Marx two paragraphs like these:

> The social principles of Christianity preach cowardice, self-contempt, abasement, submission, dejection, in a word all the qualities of the *canaille*; and the proletariat, not wishing to be treated as *canaille*, needs its courage, its self-feeling, its pride and its sense of independence more than its bread.
>
> The social principles of Christianity are sneakish and the proletariat is revolutionary.[6]

These paragraphs are noteworthy as indications of Marx's estimate of working men and women, but if they are used to define his estimate of Christianity, one has evidence suitable for a "friendly" witness before some Subversive Activities Control Board hearing. The paragraphs come from an essay ironically entitled "The Communism of the Paper *Rheinischer Beobachter*" (1847). Marx is polemicizing with the ultrareactionary newspaper of Cologne and with a State Councillor who had just attacked in the name of "the social principles of Christianity" what he called the fearful conspiracy of communism. In modern terms, this is a piece of irony directed against the delusions of the *New York Daily News* and J. Edgar Hoover.

One should bear in mind that when reading the books of Marx and Engels (and Lenin) one is reading books, not sacred scripts. To read these men in any manner other than a scientific one is to show contempt for them, since devotion to science was their passion.

2

Bohdan R. Bociurkiw, who makes clear his anti-Leninist views in an essay on "Lenin and Religion," purports to find a significant difference between Lenin's approach to religion and that of Marx and Engels. He writes:

Against their stressing that the disappearance of religion depends on the prior abolition of its social and economic roots, Lenin upgrades the importance of "consciousness," of the active struggle against religious ideology as a means, if not a condition, of a successful struggle against political and economic oppression.[7]

Quite apart from Bociurkiw's invidious and *ad hominem* assertions — "Clearly, Lenin's motives are those of a political strategist rather than humanitarian,"[8] or, Lenin's "early interest in manipulating religious dissent for revolutionary purposes . . . ,"[9] and so on—this presentation of an alleged difference between the Marxist and the Leninist approach to religion is excessive.

Lenin repeatedly stressed the need, in the struggle against socio-economic oppression, to overcome the attraction of and the need for religion; he certainly, also, emphasized the need for simultaneously seeking to undercut religious ideology through scientific educational effort, through enhancing "consciousness." So did Marx and Engels. It is true, however, that Lenin did stress the task of developing the consciousness related to removing or at least reducing the enormous influence of institutionalized religion among the peoples of czarist and then Soviet Russia.

There are two distinctive elements in the life of Lenin, as contrasted with those of Marx and Engels, that go far to explain their different emphases. First, Lenin was a Russian revolutionist. Second, Lenin led a successful revolution; he headed the party that had achieved this success and headed the state created thereby. He faced the problems of religion in Russia, with its Byzantine Christian church, its Asian religions, and its history of very close ties between church and state. Lenin also faced the task of establishing the first socialist society in a country whose educational and technical levels were particularly low. His efforts met fierce opposition from ruling classes and capitalist states outside Russia and from antirevolutionary forces within Russia, among which the church was prominent.

Lenin's writing is directly and wholly polemical. He was always "engaged" in a specific and immediate sense. There is, therefore, a tendency in much of his writing toward a certain exaggeration of expression that, taken out of context, can lead to distortion of its meaning. This is especially true of his writings on religion and the Orthodox church, because the state so clearly used both and because the church as such was so fierce and so foul an ally of czarism. With the defeat of the 1905 Revolution and the onset of a period of special reaction there was a tendency among both Right and ultra-Left opponents of the Bolsheviks to move in the direction of either "god-builders" and party liquidationists, or professional atheists and opponents of any activity—including parliamentary—within circles of the Establishment. Among Lenin's opponents (including men like Gorky, Lunacharsky, and Bogdanov) from both the Left and the Right, attitudes toward religion were central; hence, Lenin's writings on this question, especially from 1907 through 1913, were created as weapons for intraparty as well as general revolutionary struggles.[10]

Joseph Needham has observed that after the fall of Byzantium, the emphasis upon otherworldliness that had constituted one strand of classical Christianity "transferred itself to the Church of Russia." Hence, as Needham pointed out, that Church was devoid of the social theories that characterized so much of Western Christianity. With the appearance of capitalism in Russia, therefore, the Church assisted in "enslav[ing] a population which could make no appeal to any distinctively Christian social theories," simply because such theories had never been developed there.[11]

The established church, to which other churches paid taxes, possessed enormous wealth in capital and land, and owned hundreds of shops, apartments, and businesses. In professional and institutional capacities there were about two hundred thousand persons in its hierarchy prior to World War I. At the head of that church, as God's own appointee, sat the Czar himself.

Naturally, then, the church stood as the basic bulwark of czarism. Anything threatening the monarch aroused ecclesiastical hostility, hence the church's attitude toward socialism was to condemn it as quite literally the devil's concoction. In February 1917, just after the Czar's abdication, in the face of the "threat" of republican government and in the midst of the slaughter of World War I, the Holy Synod issued this Appeal:

> Stand as an impregnable wall around the Tsar's throne. Hasten, not out of fear, but for conscience's sake, to aid the representatives of the power of the autocrat. Let now the bell of catholicity assemble all Russia under a united, great, holy banner upon which with flaming words will be written: "For the Faith, the Tsar, and the Fatherland."[12]

Only on the basis of this background can one begin to comprehend Lenin on religion.

In December of the fateful year 1905, Lenin published a fairly long essay on "Socialism and Religion." Taking off, as he writes, from "present-day society," he speaks of religion as "one of the forms of spiritual oppression which everywhere weighs down heavily upon the masses of people, overburdened by their perpetual work for others, by want and isolation." In this essay, Lenin makes perfectly clear that he refers to Russia and to its church; in this connection he calls for the complete separation of state and church, adding that "by no means can we consider religion as a private affair so far as our Party is concerned."[13]

Lenin also notes here that some of the clergy "are joining in the demand for freedom, are protesting against officialism," and other expressions of czarist oppression. Our party, he writes, "must lend this movement our support." Lenin added that "we do not forbid Christians and other believers in God to join our Party"; atheism is not made a condition of membership because "Unity in this really revolutionary struggle of the oppressed class for the creation of a paradise on earth is more important to us than unity of proletarian opinion on paradise in heaven."

Further, Lenin remarks that it is wrong to establish prohibitions based upon the presence of religious belief, since it is unreal to expect such belief to disappear, given the existence of oppressive social conditions; "economic slavery," he held, is "the true source of the religious humbugging of mankind." He notes also that the "fomenting of religious strife" is a main tactic of the Czar and his minions; this was manifesting itself most notoriously at the time of his writing in the "Black-Hundred pogroms."

Exaggeration appears in Lenin's writings when he treats religion, but, as I have indicated, these are to be read in terms of the time, place, circumstances, and purpose of the writings. Thus Lenin writes of ". . . one of the most odious things on earth, namely, religion . . . ," and this certainly is much too flat in terms of the Marxist approach to religion. Lenin here is writing about Tolstoy ("Tolstoy as the Mirror of the Russian Revolution" 1908), and his whole point is to show the contradictory character of Tolstoy's ideas so that in the instant case, this characterization of religion refers to Tolstoy's use of religion to obscure his own marvelous perceptions, as Lenin writes, his "most sober realism, the tearing away of all and sundry masks."

Again, in a letter to Gorky arguing against the latter's "god-building" ideas, Lenin wrote (in December 1913): "The idea of god *always* dulled 'social feelings,' always kept them dormant, always put the dead before the living because it was *always* the idea of slavery (worse even—of hopeless slavery)." But in this very same letter, a few lines earlier, Lenin had contradicted the word "always," which he himself underlined, for he wrote: "There was a time in history when the struggle of the democrats and the proletariat was conducted in the form of *one religious* idea against another, despite the origin and real significance of the idea of god" (Lenin's italics).

In a somewhat different case, writing "On the Significance of Militant Materialism" (1922), and noting the positive features of the separation of church and state in the United States (though, he adds, it is not complete there), he goes on to write that "so-called 'modern democracy' . . . is *nothing* but the freedom to preach that which is to the advantage of the bourgeoisie, namely, the most reactionary ideas, religion, obscurantism, defense of the exploiters, etc." Lenin here underlined "nothing," yet had he written something like "is fundamentally" or "is basically" rather than "is *nothing,*" he would have been more accurate and more in keeping with the totality of his own thought. Polemicizing and striving for the greatest posible impact in his speech and writing, Lenin did not always successfully avoid or, no doubt, want to avoid hyperbole.

Perhaps the fullest essay by Lenin devoted to religion is "The Attitude of the Workers' Party to Religion," first published in 1909. This is an all-out attack upon religion in terms of its idealist philosophic foundation contrasted with the materialist foundation of Marxism; it is a devastating critique of institutionalized religion insofar as it has played the role, historically, of the bulwark of an offensive status quo. In this essay, nevertheless, Lenin emphasizes that the struggle against religion must in no case be marked by the prohibition of religious practice and belief. It must, on the contrary, be one of argument, persuasion, and education, and above all of active struggle against those abominable social conditions whose existence is at the root of religious tendency.

It is in this essay in particular, that Lenin draws distinctions between the history and the reality of religion and church and state as these appeared in Russia and in Western Europe (and in the United States). The movement for church-state separation, Lenin points out, was bourgeois-led in Western Europe; in Russia it was a demand of the working class. Further, the church and its priests were more reactionary on the whole in Russia than in Western Europe, hence distinctions in their approach toward religion are inevitable and proper for Marxist parties in Western Europe as compared with such a party in Russia.

Lenin here argues against the "pseudo-revolutionary idea that religion should be prohibited in socialist society." Religion must be considered as a private matter so far as the state is concerned; but not, he added, so far as the party and Marxism are concerned; here serious differences exist and must not be hidden. Prohibition of religion, he emphasizes—as did Marx and Engels—is wrong and, in any case, ineffective. The need is to eliminate "the social roots of religion," and what are they? Lenin enumerates "ruin, destruction, pauperism, prostitution, death from starvation—such is *the root* of modern religion." To fight successfully against religion, one must struggle "against the blind destructive forces of capitalism, until those masses themselves learn to fight this *root* of religion, fight *the rule of capital* in all its forms, in a united, organized, planned and conscious way."

In emphasizing the differences between Western Europe and Russia concerning religion, Lenin remarks that a priest might well wish to join the Marxist party in the former, though even there it would not be a frequent phenomenon, while in Russia "it is hardly probable." Even in Russia, however, "If a priest comes to us to take part in our common political work and conscientiously performs Party duties, without opposing the Program of the Party, he may be allowed to join. . . ."

Lenin makes another distinction between Western Europe and Russia relative to religion. After noting that in the former, separation of church and state is largely a fact and it resulted from the efforts of the bourgeoisie, while in Russia separation does not exist and to accomplish it is the task of the working class, he adds two considerations. In Western Europe, the bourgeois-led battle against clericalism induced a specific "Left" distortion, namely, the anarchistic "revolutionary phrasemongering" that really "takes its stand on the bourgeois world outlook." Naturally, then, Marxist parties faced with such a situation will and must react differently from a Marxist party in Russia, where such attacks upon religion do not occur. Further, in the West, says Lenin, bourgeois governments themselves have been known to use anticlericalism and antireligious propaganda as lightning rods to distract attention from what is on their agenda—namely, working-class power and socialism. In Germany, Marxists, as is "quite understandable and legitimate," found it necessary "to counteract bourgeois and Bismarckian anti-clericalism by *subordinating* the struggle against religion to the struggle for socialism." Again Lenin adds, "In Russia conditions are different."[14]

Despite the particularly reactionary nature and role of the church in Russia and considerable "Left" pressure for harsh antireligious measures and postures, Lenin maintained the classical Marxist position of denouncing religious persecution. In his 1909 essay on "The Attitude of the Workers' Party to Religion," he wrote:

It would be a profound mistake to think that the seeming "moderation" of Marxism in regard to religion is due to supposed "tactical" considerations, the desire "not to scare away" anybody, and so forth. On the contrary, in this question, too, the political line of Marxism is inseparably bound up with its philosophical principles.

With power, Lenin maintained this position. Thus, speaking in November 1918 before the First All-Russia Congress of Working Women, he warned: "We must be extremely careful in fighting religious prejudices; some people cause a lot of harm in this struggle by offending religious feelings." Basically, Lenin added—and this was why only "moderation" would do—"The deepest source of religious prejudice is poverty and ignorance; and that is the evil we have to combat."

Soon after the Eighth Congress of the Communist Party of Soviet Russia, Bukharin and Preobrazhensky issued a semiofficial exposition of its Program (adopted in March 1919); here one may conveniently find the full text of that Program.[15] Two paragraphs are particularly relevant:

With regard to religion, the Russian Communist Party is not content with having already decreed the separation of the church from the State and of the school from the church, that is, with having taken measures which bourgeois democracy includes in its programs but has nowhere carried out owing to the manifold associations that actually obtain between capital and religious propaganda.

The Russian Communist Party is guided by the conviction that nothing but the fulfillment of purposiveness and full awareness in all the social and economic activities of the masses can lead to the complete disappearance of religious prejudices. The Party endeavors to secure the complete break-up of the union between the exploiting classes and the organizations for religious propaganda, thus cooperating in the actual deliverance of the working masses from religious prejudices, and organizing the most extensive propaganda of scientific enlightenment and anti-religious conceptions. While doing this, we must carefully avoid anything that can wound the

16

feelings of believers, for such a method can only lead to the strengthening of religious fanaticism.[16]

The authors themselves are too flat in their condemnation of religion as such, making no distinctions between institutions and feelings and none at all among different religious outlooks. They tend toward accepting in a rather vulgar way the "religion is opium" idea cited earlier. Even so, the specific reference to Russia permeates the book; thus one reads that it is "essential at the present time to wage with the utmost vigor the war against religious prejudices, for the church has now definitely become a counter-revolutionary organization."[17] The authors do not fail to add that this must be done "with patience and considerateness" to minimize giving affront.

In closing a discussion of Lenin's views on religion, one should note that the Soviet journal, *Nauka i Religia* (*Science and Religion*), in its October 1965 issue felt called upon to criticize some persons in the USSR who were urging a more "resolute" struggle against religion. The editors recalled that N. K. Krupskaya noted in her *Memoirs* that, "Ilyich used to say ... how harmful was superficial, aggressive anti-religious propaganda every sort of vulgarization."

The same journal reprinted two notes drafted by Lenin in 1921. One, written in April (the exact day is not known), was addressed to V. M. Molotov and said, in full:

> If my memory does not deceive me, the press carried a letter or circular of the C.C. [Central Committee] in connection with May 1, which says: *expose the* LIE *of religion,* or something similar.
> This will not do. This is tactless. Precisely, in connection with Easter, something *else* should be recommended:
> not "expose the lie,"
> but *avoid, absolutely, any sort of affront to religion.*
> A supplementary letter or circular needs to be published. If the Secretariat does not agree, then take it up in the Politburo.

The next month, on May 18, 1921, Lenin submitted a "Proposal Relating to Draft for CPSU(b) Plenum on Point 13 of the Party

17

Program," that is, the point dealing with religion in the 1919 Program. It reads:

> Ask Yaroslavsky and Bukharin to modify in such a way as not to highlight the question of struggle against religion . . . and to allow, along with other specifically restrictive conditions, membership in the party on the part of believers, known as honest and devoted communists.
>
> The struggle with religion to be placed in a more scientific manner.[18]

Lenin's call for the avoidance of vulgarity and the exercise of sensitivity, and his insistence that Marxism's case must be argued scientifically and determined historically, recalls, from the opposite view, the plea by Pope John XXIII in his encyclical on world peace for sensitivity toward all, including nonbelievers, and for dialogue "between believers and those who do not believe or believe insufficiently" as a means towards "discovering truth and paying homage to it."

3

Having indicated something of the Marxist approach to religion and certain sources of its distortion, let us briefly face the question of tactics.

Pressures for change on the part of religious institutions and religiously inclined people in their attitudes toward Marxism and socialism are numerous and great. Simultaneously, pressures dictating a change in attitude on the part of Marxists toward such institutions and such feelings are consequential.

The great religions face the fact that socialism is the form of society in one-third of the world, that it exists now in Asia, in Europe, in Latin America, and is being consciously sought in Africa. These religions also recognize that additional scores of millions of peoples in countries not yet socialist adhere to such a more or less avowedly Marxist perspective. This is true in Japan and France, in India and Italy, in Brazil and Finland, and in Chile and Burma.

The great religions also see that some of the most gifted and most sensitive human beings of the past fifty years have chosen the socialist path with, again, more or less explicitly Marxist features; this is true of Einstein and Aragon, of Du Bois and Amado, of Nexö and Gorki, of Picasso and Siqueiros, of Bernal and Dreiser, of Neruda and Guillen. . . .

They face the fact, too, that movements of national liberation, often with significant socialist overtones, are sweeping the colonial and semicolonial world. The Negro freedom movement in the United States also carries fundamental challenges to the structure of the social order; that movement and the responses to it today represent the most urgent challenges faced by religion and religious organizations in the United States since the pre–Civil War period.

Furthermore, all these globe-shaking developments are ensconced within and causally connected to the great scientific, demographic, and technical revolutions and innovations of the past two generations that in one way or another challenge the traditional concepts of religion.

The old order of capitalism responds to these challenges with the threat or the practice of fascism and war. Whatever may have been the policies of concession and adjustment, or even, at times, support, vouchsafed fascism by religious institutions, these policies were usually grudging or shamefaced and more or less coerced. Perhaps it will be agreed that in any case such policies of concession and/or support are regretted in hindsight.

The unprecedented challenge of general war with thermonuclear and bacterial and chemical weapons (and other horrors still on the drawing boards), presenting the real possibility of the extermination of man, induces reconsiderations of tactics vis-à-vis other human beings and other social orders no matter what their character. This involves not only such philosophical questions as the possibility of a just war using such weapons—and no religion condones any but a just war, whatever the excuses may be—but also such questions as the very persistence of religion itself. The impact of these considerations may be illustrated by the fact that in the Roman Catholic church all the post–World War II popes have expressed repeated and intense preoccupation with the necessity of peaceful coexistence among states with different social systems.

19

VIEWS AND PROBLEMS: AN INTRODUCTION

It is becoming increasingly clear to religious people of any sensitivity that persistence in opposing the worldwide demand for an end to hunger, illiteracy, and indignity is suicidal. The Canadian Catholic philosopher, Leslie Dewart, has argued this persuasively in *Christianity and Revolution: The Lesson of Cuba*, particularly in the chapter, "The Theology of Counter-Revolution."[19]

The considerations offered above as inducing alteration in the attitude expressed by religious institutions and people toward Marxism also work the other way, that is, they also induce changes in attitude and conduct from Marxists relative to religious institutions and people. Where socialism exists it is necessary to deal constructively and decently with the inhabitants of such lands. This must be done in countries having different religions and different traditions, even if the formal religions are the same. Problems and considerations differ, that is, not only in terms of traditionally Protestant sections of Czechoslovakia as contrasted with traditionally Catholic areas, but also between the Catholic church of Poland, whose tradition is allied with a prolonged national struggle, and that Church in Hungary, where its tradition has supported an intensely chauvinistic, aggressive, and anti-Semitic hierarchy.

The church in Italy must adjust to the reality of nearly two million Italians who choose to be Communists and one-fourth of the electorate who vote Communist, but so must the Communist party of Italy adjust to the fact that thousands of its members belong to the church and millions of its electoral supporters also adhere to the church.

With the advent of fascism in Germany, the entire outlook of the world Communist movement shifted, as symbolized in Dimitrov's Report to the VII Congress (1935) of the Communist International. This outlook remains basically in effect; it is an outlook of breadth and unity, shunning sectarianism and narrowness. It is an outlook of unity with all who stand opposed to fascism and war, unity with all such persons no matter what other differences may be present.

It was in response to this threat on the international level that the worldwide Communist movement developed the policy of collective security; this remains in effect in a new, wider, and more urgent form as the necessity for peaceful coexistence among states having

20

different social systems. It remains and is emphasized because the danger of war persists and because the nature of another general war will certainly be catastrophic and may quite well be annihilating.

These are the essential reasons why all of us—whatever our motivations and truths, religious or scientific, spiritual or material —must act together for great ends and must discuss our differences with dignity and with a predetermination not to aggravate them but to delimit them, clarify them, and, hopefully, to learn from that process. This does not mean abandoning outlooks, unless one is persuaded of a superior vision, but it does mean recognizing the mutual necessity for respect and regard.

It is vital that fanaticism be avoided and that there be appreciation for the necessity that flexibility be encouraged and that change and growth be assumed. Truth advances through the detection of error; error is detected through reason and through science (and, others may add, through revelation). To one who thinks, there is no greater service than the detection of error.

Marxism and religion have existed together for over a century. If Marxism is correct, and if the universal achievement of communism produces a world that is reasonable and controllable and therefore a world in which religion, being unnecessary, will disappear, why, then, that is what will happen. If, on the other hand, this Marxist projection is wrong—and, of course, it may well be wrong —then religion will not disappear and perhaps will never disappear. In either case the worst that can happen is that one of the two, the religious person or the Marxist, will have been proven in error. Each, then, will be wiser. Is that a calamity?

Not only will each be wiser; both will be alive. It is commonly said that given the will, one may find the way. Surely we may also say that, given life, mankind will find solutions. If it be replied, not solutions—or that solutions in any ultimate sense are impossible— one may reply that he thinks otherwise but that perhaps this view is correct. Let us then agree that given life, man may always seek solutions.

Chapter Two

Openings

Among the most recent and challenging of the Marxist-Christian dialogue books is one published in 1969. Edited by Thomas W. Ogletree, a professor of theology at Chicago Theological Seminary, *Openings for Marxist-Christian Dialogue* contains essays by the editor and Jürgen Moltmann of the University of Tubingen in the German Federal Republic, Charles C. West of Princeton Theological Seminary, Paul Lehmann of Union Theological Seminary in New York, and by Sidney Lens of Chicago.[1]

These men are learned and fair-minded; not one, however, is a Marxist, and so while the book to which they contribute is meant to suggest "openings" for a dialogue between Marxists and Christians, the absence of the former is an unfortunate limitation. My intention in this chapter and the next is to enter the opening for a dialogue with the authors of *Openings*. To engage in this dialogue it will be necessary for me to quote at some length and to paraphrase; this is perhaps clumsy for the reader but still will bring the actual dialogue directly to him. For the entirety of the views being discussed, readers will of course go to the original source. As in most dialogues, points of difference in view or understanding will be emphasized, thus tending to obscure areas of general agreement. But before this volume is completed such areas will have not only appeared but will have been emphasized. To the "openings," then. Ogletree writes in his introduction:

> While religion has on occasion been associated with genuine revolutionary movements, Marx and Engels still considered it to be primarily a barrier to human progress. On the one hand, it causes the downtrodden to acquiesce in the face of oppression and exploitation, to seek the fulfillment of life not in a real struggle for historical change, but in an illusory world created by the religious imagination. "Religion is the opium of the people." Engels noted how frequently the European bourgeoisie, following the uprisings of 1848, insisted that "religion must be kept alive for the masses. Experience had taught them that religion has a strong stabilizing influence on workers and peasants."

Ogletree continues with an example from British history in the nineteenth century of bourgeois subsidization of a religious revivalist effort, and then concludes:

> On the other hand, religion provides a sacral legitimation for the established order, no matter how just or unjust it may be. Paul's own words quite aptly illustrate Marx's point: "Let every person be subject to the governing authorities. For there is no authority except from God, and those that exist have been instituted by God. Therefore, he who resists the authorities resists what God has appointed." (Rom. 13:1—2). Because religion is characteristically allied with the present order, an attack on social evils necessarily involves an attack on religious authority as well. Marx once observed that criticism of religion is the beginning of all criticism. His point is that once we are free to challenge sacral authority, we are free to challenge any kind of social arrangement which oppresses or alienates men. Under these circumstances, the final liberation of man from economic exploitation and political oppression requires his liberation from religion itself.[2]

Ogletree's summary of the situation seems on the whole less than exact. It is not that Marxism considers religion a barrier to human progress; rather, Marxism considers religion a reflection of the level of a particular social order. To the extent that religion has been a "reflection," religious institutions can be, have been, and are now being used in most times and places to sustain the status quo; in other circumstances religious feeling has been and is an inspirational source justifying and encouraging challenges to the status

24

quo. The distinction between religious feeling and religious institutions, crucial to the Marxist approach to the question of religion, tends to be ignored by Ogletree.

Ogletree's presentation falters, too, because it presents the Marxist view statically, that is, as though Marx and Engels viewed religion as a rather distinct thing in and of itself. But Marx and Engels never viewed any object or process statically; and certainly so long-enduring and so dynamic a phenomenon as religion can only be caricatured if it is examined as a thing in itself. Essential, however, to the Marxist approach in general, and its approach to religion in particular, is that Marxism views religion in terms of time and place and circumstance, and in terms of class differentiations. In this sense, the use of the "opium" quotation is quite deficient.

Paul is accurately quoted, of course, by Ogletree, but there are other holy figures in the Bible and other passages that teach quite different things than this particular citation from Paul. And it is these other passages, often containing dissident and even revolutionary arguments, that appealed to people like John Brown, Nat Turner, Harry F. Ward, and A. J. Muste; they were not the less "religious" for having such a message and such an appeal.

Marx's point about the significance of the criticism of religion is not properly rendered when one presents Marx as viewing such criticism as "the beginning of all criticism." Marx said such criticism was the "premise" of all criticism, not the beginning, because, —in the very work from which the "opium" quotation comes— "For Germany the *criticism of religion* is in the main complete, and criticism of religion is the premise of all criticism." That is, assuming Feuerbach and his demonstration that man himself makes religion and that God is created in man's image (and not the other way around), one must move forward from that "premise" and see, as Marx continues, that "religion is the self-consciousness and self-feeling of man who has either not yet found himself or has already lost himself again."

(It is following this line of thought that Marx's two paragraphs —including the one with the "opium" remark—occur and they have been quoted earlier. There it has been argued that any reading of the section in its entirety makes quite inadequate the traditional

25

view—repeated by Ogletree—that this passage means simply that Marx views religion as a force that "causes the downtrodden to acquiesce.")

Marx's point is *not* that "once we are free to challenge sacral authority, we are free to challenge any kind of social arrangement which oppresses or alienates man." It is, rather, that social arrangements (and human knowledge) are of such a character (and at such a level) that sacral authority is *needed*, and therefore it appears and is supported. Further, Marxism holds that as knowledge of the faulty and regressive character of social arrangement grows and effective alternatives appear, and as knowledge of nature develops, the religious need diminishes; the challenge to the sacral reflects the challenge to the secular and each reacts upon the other.

Ogletree writes that "the final liberation of man from economic exploitation and political oppression requires his liberation from religion itself"; it is more accurate to say that both movements would occur simultaneously and reinforce each other and spring from the same basic source: an awareness of an increasingly deficient socioeconomic order (part of which awareness comes from the growing conquest of nature and its secrets). All this, Marxism believes, makes cumulatively irrelevant the superstructure reflecting and bulwarking that order; important here, though overlooked in this instance by Ogletree, is the development of science with its tendency to diminish the intensity of the need for religion.

This latter process was fundamental to the secularization of thought in the eighteenth and nineteenth centuries; its impact has certainly not lessened in the twentieth. Dietrich Bonhoeffer, in his *Letters and Papers from Prison*, had this in mind when he remarked that "God is no longer necessary as a working hypothesis"; the point is expressed with clarity by Charles C. West in *Communism and the Theologians:* "That realm of nature which used to be beyond human understanding and control with which, therefore, one could only establish a creative relation by means of this hypothesis 'God,' is now more and more conquered by reason and technique."[3]

Basic, too, to the Marxist view of religion and its function—as feeling but not as institution—is the awareness that this is a need felt by all classes, and that these classes respond differently in terms of what religion *is* and what function it performs *for them;* what ruling classes may want need not be what they actually get.

Ogletree offers another opportunity for dialogue when he writes:

> Given their understanding of the essentially regressive role of religion, Marx and Engels would have found little sense in a dialogue with Christian theologians. Even if such dialogue produced no harmful results, it would at least be a diversion from the business at hand. At best, religion is a useless encumbrance destined to pass away with man's "coming of age." At worst it is a barrier to human progress which must be vigorously opposed.[4]

This passage again reflects a tendency to confuse religious institution and feeling, as indicated in its remark that Marx and Engels would have seen no point in conversing with Christian *theologians;* surely these are not the only Christians, not to speak of the only people who are religious. As we hope has been shown in earlier pages, Marx and Engels certainly did not view religion "at best" as a "useless encumbrance," for surely that which is needed and which supplies perfume in a world otherwise stinking to heaven is neither useless nor an encumbrance.

At its worst—for instance, as handmaiden to the Czar's power and rule or as an instrument to sustain the present regime in South Africa—religion is certainly to be "vigorously opposed," but even there what is to be vigorously opposed is the *institution.*[5] Part of the opposition is an insistence that such use of religion is contrary to the heart of the original religious impulse. The kind of preaching denounced in the remarks of James Maurer quoted earlier is the kind of "understanding of religion and God, and man's resultant relation to him and to an after-life, [which] is a betrayal and misrepresentation of much of Christ's message," as a Roman Catholic priest has recently written.[6]

When Marx and Engles lived and worked they would have been hard put to find a theologian in Europe who would have conversed with them! Many theologians today, in the words of Helmut Gollwitzer, see the birth and appeal of Marxism as "a bill for our

27

[Christians] neglects." Charles West, again makes this point with great force:

It is the disgrace of Christian theology that Marx found in it, not the Gospel of Good news to the whole man, body and soul, especially to the humble and the poor, not the promise of the coming of an already risen and ruling Christ, but only the division of body from spirit, the hope of a spiritual eternal life, and the neglect or the sanctification of the material arrangements of this world.[7]

Ogletree explains "the significance of the current readiness of Marxist philosophers to dialogue with Christian theologians," on the basis "that it constitutes an acknowledgement of the presence of theological considerations in Marxist thought and a recognition that Marxism has in part functioned in a manner that is equivalent to a religious perspective."[8]

I do not know for which Marxists Ogletree speaks; he does not speak for this one, and my engagement in such dialogue has by no means been a matter of yesterday's labors. The significance of the current readiness for dialogue on the part of Marxist philosophers with Christian theologians lies first in the fact that there are many theologians who now welcome such dialogue, and many others who at least do not actively oppose it. In the second place, the theologians' willingness to talk reflects the crisis in religion—in society—and the deep and growing conviction in religious institutions and groups that encounter with the world and service to man on this earth is the church's duty and need.

We may call to witness, as one example among what in our day constitutes a veritable cloud of such witnesses, the words issuing from the World Council's Conference on Church and Society, held in Geneva in July 1966. In its section on "A Theological Understanding of Social Change" occurs a passage that consciously or otherwise, actually paraphrases Marx in his famous declaration: "The philosophers have only *interpreted* the world in various ways; the point however is to *change* it" (Marx's italics).[9] The World Council affirmed that Christianity

remains a discipline which aims not at a theoretical system of truth but at action in human society. Its object is not simply to understand the world,

28

but to respond to the power of God which is recreating it. .... Christian theology is prophetic only in so far as it dares, in full reflection, to declare how, at a particular place and time, God is at work, and thus to show the Church where and when to participate in his work.[10]

Of the "nine propositions for Christian action" that said the official report, "seem to emerge from the Conference," the first two were:

The alleviation of human suffering and achievement of the abundant life for all. .... This must include energetic work towards the elimination of the social causes of suffering as well as care for the victims of injustice and misfortune.

and

The concern for just relationships in society is one aspect of the compassionate ministry. This passion for equity in political, social and economic structures has both a preventive and healing function.[11]

No wonder, then, that the conference said: "Specifically we urge that the World Council of Churches seek to initiate an informal dialogue with Marxists, on an international basis, in each region of the world."

It is difficult to believe that under such circumstances, "Marx and Engels would have found little sense in a dialogue with Christian theologians." The current readiness, then, among Marxist philosophers to engage in dialogue is explained to a considerable extent by developments among theologians. As for "the presence of theological considerations in Marxist thought," yes, if such considerations are defined in the terms brought forward by Vatican II and the 1966 conference of the World Council of Churches. And as for Marxism functioning in part in a way similar to a religious perspective, again, yes, if that perspective is defined in terms such as those quoted from the 1966 conference.

The current readiness among Marxists for dialogue with theologians stems, too, from another consideration brought forward by that conference, namely, "the furtherance of peace and progress for all mankind"[12]; it stems also from sources that Ogletree may have been too kind to mention. These include the shattering blows that

29

Marxist philosophers have suffered from the aberrations, crimes, and failures that have marked the course of the history of socialism; those who remain Marxists have not, obviously, interpreted these failures as a total discrediting of Marxism. On the contrary, the positive accomplishments of socialism where it has been in power for the past half century and the efforts and accomplishments inspired by Marxism in the rest of the world have, in my opinion, more than vindicated the essential genius of Marx and the basic insights of Marxism.

But the blows have been there and have required reexamination; for such reexamination nothing is more helpful than the rigor of dialogue. Socialism has appeared in a large part of the world now; its form has varied within particular countries and will do so in the future, since new problems and circumstances will appear; it has varied, too, at any given moment, from one region to another. If it had not, Marxism would be hard put to explain such uniformity! At the same time, the variations themselves also have induced hard rethinking. Nothing is more healthy for any mental discipline than such challenges. To have the opportunity of talking with others whose point of vision is different can only be helpful. In more urgent and widespread form than ever before in the history of Marxism (or in history as a whole), basic questions confront us about the nature of man, the purpose of existence, sources of alienation, and uses of power. All serious systems of thought, including religions, have devoted much energy to these matters, and for Marxists to get the benefit of these efforts through direct conversation can only be helpful.

There are points of difference that must be brought forward concerning Ogletree's discussion of the Marxist view on the permanency of religion. He seems to believe that Marx held that religion's existence was to be shortlived in the face of developments experienced in the nineteenth century and those projected for the following century. Thus, Ogletree writes: "... modern developments in scientific and social thinking have not brought about the demise of religion as Marx and Engels anticipated."[13]

Evidence has earlier been presented showing that Marx did not see the possibility of the demise of religion until the mysteries of nature as a whole had been resolved and until the antagonisms and contradictions in human relationships had been overcome; hence, clearly, the view expressed by Ogletree is inexact, though common. It must be added that while the developments he refers to have not resulted in the demise of religion, surely it will be agreed that they have contributed to the decline of religion, and this is in accordance with the Marxist projection.

Ogletree moves from this inexactitude to more serious error when he writes: "The realistic Marxist thinker finds it necessary to reflect critically on the fact that religion may have an enduring role in human experience, a fact that necessitates a revision of the traditional Marxist analysis of religion."[14] Here Ogletree is moving much too rapidly from what he himself feels "may" be true, to the assumption that it is true, or has been established, and is therefore a "fact" that must induce revision in Marxist thinking.

He goes on at once to suggest that the reappraisal he says this necessitates has already commenced. Thus he writes: "The 'Testament' of Palmiero Togliatti, the late General Secretary of the Italian Communist Party, reflects such a reappraisal." And then he quotes Harvey Cox's quotation from Togliatti:

The old atheistic propaganda is of no use. The very problem of religious conscience, its content, its roots among the masses, and the way of overcoming it must be presented in a different manner from that adopted in the past if we wish to reach the Catholic masses and be understood by them. Otherwise our outstretched hand to the Catholics would be regarded as pure expediency and almost as hypocrisy.

Note that this quotation is offered as evidence that Marxists recognize the necessity of revising traditional concepts that affirmed the early demise of religion. But if the entire paragraph in which occurs the quoted matter from Togliatti is examined, it has quite a different meaning. The omitted beginning of Togliatti's paragraph reads:

In the organized Catholic world and among the mass of the Catholics there was a clear move to the Left during the time of Pope John. There has now been a swing back to the Right at the center. At the base, however, there persists the conditions and the pressure for a move to the Left which

31

we must understand and assist. For this purpose the old atheist propaganda is of no use.[15]

Togliatti is not here announcing a revision of the Marxist view of religion in the light of an alleged "fact" of its permanence, contrary to an alleged Marxist concept of its great fragility. Knowing as he did the problems of Communist-Catholic unity on action —and the rejection of such an offer made in the 1930s by the Italian Communist party, then illegal under fascism—Togliatti is urging that "the old atheist propaganda" of the fascist era is worse than useless in the present era, considering the changes in Italy—not least the end of fascism—and in Catholicism (to Pope John XXIII and from Pope John to Pope Paul VI, but with a continuing Left impulse down below). Togliatti goes on to say that such basic changes demand fundamental tactical alterations; the latter require a more profound comprehension of the significance and role of religious feeling among the masses of Italian people. Even in this context, note also that Togliatti is talking about "the way of overcoming it," i.e., this feeling or "conscience," insofar as that may block effective and practical unity among Communists and others. Nothing here reflects agreement on the part of this "realistic Marxist thinker" as to religion's "enduring role in human experience."

Ogletree also affirms that "the traditional Marxist critique of religion" held it to be at best a phenomenon that "sometimes functions as a disguise for tangible, earthly interests in a revolutionary struggle"[16]; in this sense he hails Garaudy's view, which "suggests that religion may be a *contributing factor,* an enabler, in that struggle."

Marx and Engels did not treat religion as a disguise for revolutionary impulses, certainly not if one uses the word disguise in any invidious sense. They did insist upon socioeconomic and historic sources as basic to revolutionary development and effort; in that sense they treated any philosophical or ideological justification for such movements as "disguise," i.e., as a consciousness of the material substratum and, therefore, as a kind of "disguise."

Here, for example, is Engels writing of the anti-Church establishment thinking—the heretical thinking—that marked the era he described in *The Peasant War in Germany:*

It demanded the restoration of early Christian equality among members of the community and the recognition of this equality as a prescript for the burgher world as well. From "equality of the children of God" it inferred civil equality, and partly even equality of property. Equality of nobleman and peasant, of patrician, privileged burgher and plebeian, abolition of the *corvée*, ground-rents, taxes, privileges, and at least the most crying differences in property—those were the demands advanced with more or less determination as natural implications of the early Christian doctrine.

The point in all this is not a matter of disguise, but a matter of effective presentation and an awareness that religious concepts, images, and modes of thought were universal and dominant and therefore not only natural but also most persuasive. When Nat Turner, in a Virginia jail in 1831, tells his court-appointed interrogator—who demands of the slave rebel an admission that his effort at insurrection had been "wrong"—"Was not Christ crucified?," no Marxist would for a moment infer or believe this to have been a disguise. On the contrary, it was a passionately held conviction of deepest justification, and it was, without any doubt, "a contributing factor, an enabler," to use Ogletree's words.

There is a final area of disagreement with Ogletree's presentation; this has to do with his tendency—less marked than is true of many other writers—to make of Marxism a materialist view, in the near-vulgar sense of that term. He does not quite accuse it of being economic determinist—apparently this falsification is fading away, at least in scholarly circles—but he does, I think, minimize its complexity and subtlety.[17]

Ogletree writes, for example, that "Marxism has so emphasized the fact that man is a creature constituted by social relationships, that it has tended to assume all human difficulties would be removed by a reordering of the structure of society"[18]; or, "Marx's thought was too simplistic in linking both man's suffering and his hope to the economic and political structures of human society"[19]; or, while Marxism's apprehension of the presence of alienation was helpful, it chose "to trace the alienation solely to a certain manner or ordering of the productive relations of society."[20]

33

Engels himself notes:

Marx and I are ourselves partly to blame for the fact that the younger writers sometimes lay more stress on the economic side than is due to it. We had to emphasize this main principle in opposition to our adversaries, who denied it, and we had not always the time, the place or the opportunity to allow the other elements involved in the interaction to come into their rights.

In their own lifetimes, both Marx and Engels already felt it necessary to denounce vulgarizers, those who, to quote Engels, "simply make use of the phrase historical materialism (and *every-thing* can be turned into a phrase), in order to get their own relatively scanty historical knowledge ... fitted together into a neat system as quickly as possible...." Marx, who well knew the meaning of laborious research, excoriated the "simpletons" who felt that the answers were ready at hand and "whose inspiration comes 'from above.'" Exhausting search and excruciating thought were not for them: "Why should the innocents bother their heads about economics and history?" To them, "everything is so simple." Yes, "everything is so simple!" Marx exploded. "In their heads perhaps, the simpletons."[21]

Marx and Engels nowhere in their writing assume or tend to assume that "all human difficulties would be removed by a reordering of society," and both in their own lives had enough difficulties to know that such simplification was absurd. They did affirm that certain "difficulties"—ranging from starvation to treating colored peoples as worse than dogs—could be successfully overcome with social reordering, and they did project the idea that with such reordering the transformation of human behavior in terms of greater solidarity and fraternity would become possible. And they did insist that the main—the ultimate—(not the sole) requirement to achieve such possibilities lay in transforming the relations of production that, they held, basically determined the character of a social order. Linking certain of man's sufferings—as poverty and illiteracy—and certain of man's hopes—as security and learning—to the economic and political structures is in Marx and Engels and has been refuted by no one and by no experience since they projected their ideas.

Nowhere does Marx trace his view of alienation solely to a particular form of production relation; he sees the root of such alienation in capitalist commodity production, and the possibility of overcoming or diminishing that alienation both by participation in the struggle to revolutionize forms of production and by restructuring the whole labor process and the whole tone of life after revolution. Marx by no means ignored questions of mechanization, of industrialization and urbanization, of specialization, or of anonymity; nor did he project that socialism would eliminate the human problems involved therein. He did believe that socialism would provide a base whose character favored efforts at their elimination and that—especially with the "higher form" of socialism, communism, success would be achieved.

On the basis of the history of the past fifty years, observers differ as to the validity of these insights and the degree of successes achieved in practice, but this means at least two things: Experience has not disproven Marx's views on the roots of alienation and the means of overcoming it; secondly, the experience is quite limited (for at its most mature it is but fifty years old, and even then has been encumbered and challenged by so many other considerations, for example, World War II and the killing of over twenty million Soviet citizens) and therefore to conclude that Marxism is "too simplistic" is both to ignore the content of its literature and to come to judgments prematurely.

These matters are of consequence in themselves but they become of decisive importance when, on the basis of his readings of Marx, Ogletree writes:

> Because the communist movement does not acknowledge the moral contradictions that accompany every level of social advance, but thinks it can bring into being a society that overcomes alienation and oppression, it considers itself fully justified in using any means to realize its aims. . . .[22]

No source is offered for these opinions; I think because none—from the "communist movement," that is, or from Marxism—can be found. Certainly Marxism not only acknowledges the moral contradictions that accompany every level of social advance, it points to them, as for example, in the limitations of the English, American, French, and 1848 Revolutions, or in the American Civil War and its aftermath, or in the Bolshevik Revolution itself, as Lenin's writings from 1917 to his death make clear.

Nor did Marx and Engels, nor has any Communist party at any time affirmed that the "use of any means whatever to realize its aims" is justified. Even if one quotes Lenin concerning what may be necessary for revolutionary fighters facing the Czar and his repression, one will not find there the justification of any means in such a resistance. As a philosophical principle, Marxism holds to the integral relationship between means and ends; if the latter are antihuman and foul, they besmirch the former. I am not saying here that foul means have not been resorted to by Communists, and I do not refer to the "normal" activity associated with engaging in war; I am rather referring to atrocities committed by those calling themselves Communists. To generalize from such instances—always denounced when exposed and known within the Communist movement—is equivalent to the kind of undifferentiated denunciation of Christianity that fills a genre of one-sided literature which confuses institutionalized Christianity with the whole religion and then devotes itself only to the worst features of the former. Thus Homer Smith, a professor of physiology at the New York University College of Medicine, writes:

> Self-mortification, squalor and physical uncleanliness became esteemed Christian virtues. . . . Christianity undermined the family . . . by teaching that celibacy is an exalted virtue; . . . It supplanted courage and initiative by resignation . . . it obliterated education and experience from ethics . . . it paralyzed all curiosity and intelligent examination of the natural world . . . for the sense of the dignity of man . . . it substituted the doctrine of personal inadequacy, the sense of guilt, and the habits of self-doubt and self-abnegation. In its cardinal doctrine of sin, . . . it promulgated a belief which was to crucify the whole of the Western world for centuries to come.[23]

I think Ogletree would argue that this is not a full and accurate rendering of Christianity, though Smith is well able in his book to document every assertion from some portion of sacred writing and some well-founded record of church activity; I would agree with Ogletree. Ogletree is not nearly as harsh toward Marxism and communism as Smith is toward Christianity; but many others are, and this is one of the great obstacles facing both him and me in common aspirations toward effective dialogue. Hence, asserting— with no documentation, since none is available—that "the communist movement" justifies the use of any means whatsoever to gain its ends (however the latter are defined, whether in the relatively sympathetic terms of Ogletree or in the fanatically hostile terms of J. Edgar Hoover) opens Pandora's box and makes most difficult the pursuit of reasonable discourse. It follows logically from a certain rigidity and deterministic simplicity that, as has been shown, Ogletree attributes to Marxism; both the attribution and the conclusion drawn from it do not accord with the reality of Marxism, in theory or in life.

It is in fact necessary to say, and a pleasure to be able to say, that Ogletree manifests generosity in his approach to Marxism. He emphasizes the corrective value of Marxism for Christianity in that it has helped force the latter to face duties and tasks on this earth and, in Marxism's concern for the wretched of the earth, has helped bring Christianity—or, at any rate, many Christians—to face that concern. He underscores the "profoundly moral content" of Marxism—despite his remark about means and ends—and feels that its atheism "deserves profound respect" since it is motivated by concern for man. While he suggests that Marxism would do well to reconsider its views on God, he also urges upon his fellow Christians, in a courageous phrase, that "dialogue with Marxists likewise requires an openness to the problematic nature of belief in God, including its possible demonic consequences in human experience."[24]

Ogletree rejects a God who serves as an excuse for inactivity or as a barrier to full human responsibility; he welcomes a God who seeks not to control man but rather to empower him—and to do so in order that man may be better able to fulfill himself. He adds a thought—already very much present, of course, in Karl Rahner— of Christianity as the religion of the future. This idea of man's openness to the future, he suggests, has played a creative role in the

37

historic process; indeed, he thinks that "man is constituted as much by his orientation to new possibilities as by the social and historic factors that shape and condition his being."[25] I suggest that these factors, shaping and conditioning his being, also condition his orientation to new possibilities; but I think, nevertheless, that this idea does project an important consideration for Marxists. As one who has labored in history, I have often been struck by the influence of the desire for immortality and the concern as to one's mark on the future upon what men do and why they do it; it does seem to me that this force rarely finds its full reflection in the chronicles of history.[26]

Partially because of the values and challenges he sees in Marxism, Ogletree offers a brief but incisive and just critique of Reinhold Niebuhr, especially in his post–World War II writings. Niebuhr's thought "has become increasingly serviceable in supporting essentially conservative social and political positions"; his "realism" (and not only his) has turned into "a handy intellectual tool to defend the interests of privileged persons and groups." This very much needs saying—and developing—and that Marxism helps evoke it from a Christian philosopher in the United States already establishes the value of dialogue![27]

Chapter Three

Widening the Opening

1

The essays in the Ogletree volume[1] by Jürgen Moltmann of the University of Tübingen in the German Federal Republic and Charles C. West of the Princeton Theological Seminary deal with basic questions in the Marxist-Christian dialogue. Both Moltmann and West find themselves obligated to speak not only for themselves but also in the name of Marxists; that is, they often contrast or compare their positions with those alleged to be held by Marxists. Once again, however, it is somewhat incongruous to present a dialogue through the mouth of only one side. Let us, then, widen the opening the Ogletree book affords and converse briefly with Moltmann and West.

Moltmann sees Christianity as a faith of renewal, power, and of hope. He rejects the widely held concept of religious faith as a condition of absolute dependence; rather, he sees it as conveying a "feeling of absolute freedom," citing well-known passages from the New Testament Gospels which assert that for him who believes, all things are possible, and that with God nothing may not be achieved. While this position leaves those who do not possess such faith or who have their doubts about the "good news" as being somewhat less than omnipotent—and such doubters or disbelievers constitute the majority of mankind—it certainly presents a view of Christianity with which the Marxist is comparatively comfortable. Moltmann notes, too, that in what is called the Old Testament, God is one who leads out of bondage; freedom comes from Him and with Him and not in opposition to Him. Here one must add that the freedom there bestowed was limited to those chosen by Him, and that those not so chosen received plague and torment rather than freedom. True, the torment was retribution dealt a tyrannical ruler, but this offered, one suspects, little comfort to the parents of the "first-born sons" who died.

If, then, it is necessary to modify Moltmann's view that "Christian proclamation is actually the religion of an exceedingly great freedom" for those who choose to be Christians, it is consequential to observe that he draws a distinction between holding that belief and the institutionalization of Christianity, for he notes that "the Christian church has often concerned itself more with authority than with this freedom."[2] To the degree that Christianity makes freedom depend upon possession of its faith, the affirmation of authority would seem to be required; this, I think, explains—or helps to explain—the manner in which Moltmann himself says the church generally has functioned. He clearly regrets the latter; but without facing the organic source for such behavior in the very belief that he embraces, he can scarcely move beyond rather impotent lamentation on this point.

Moltmann believes that with Christ, "life in history was made meaningful for the first time." The last four words here may be excessive. But the point he is making, and that Rudolf Bultmann, Harvey Cox, and others have made, is that "the past was considered as the power of sin, the future as the dynamic of grace, and the present became the time of decision."[3] While the Bible surely contains references to a past prior to the power of sin—else the Fall makes no sense at all—the dynamic quality of Christianity is Moltmann's main point, and this emphasis certainly does provide the

40

basis for kinship with Marxism. Moltmann sees the problem of freedom as essentially one of humanization; I agree, and since humanization is seen by Moltmann as a process, the agreement may be affirmed even if the actual content of that freedom is not spelled out.

One finds in Moltmann's essay the view that Marxism tends to pin its hopes of humanization only on economic progress; on the other hand, he declares—correctly, I think—that Marx's projection of a communist society was one in which *being* displaced *having*. Part of the confusion is that Moltmann identifies the Marxist view of socialism with that of communism. The former, of course, was presented by Marx and is presented in all Marxist literature and thought, as the transitional stage between capitalism and communism; the marks of capitalism upon socialism are expected to be severe and the distinctions between the socialist and the communist societies are not very much less significant, in Marxist thought, than those between capitalism and socialism.

This is related to Moltmann's thought that "The starting point of this socialist revolution lies in the disillusionary experience of the French and capitalist revolutions."[4] For the Marxist, unlike many others, there was nothing "disillusionary" in those revolutions; on the contrary, their severe limitations were confirmatory both of the Marxist analysis and of the Marxist projection of the need for the socialist revolution.

Socialism's deepest "perversions," according to Moltmann, lie "in the foreboding that the expected 'human emancipation of man' will not come automatically when the economic liberation of men in the socialist industrial state has taken place." I object, first, because the socialist state, unlike the communist one, does not bring economic liberation; it brings the termination of economic exploitation and makes possible, through social changes and technical advances, economic liberation that may be defined as the stage in which economic needs have been overcome for all. And I object, secondly, because it was never expected or asserted by Marxists that human emancipation would come "automatically" with economic liberation. Emancipation requires economic liberation and does make liberation possible, but it does not automatically bring about that emancipation. The two processes are interdependent. Moltmann concludes: "The disappointment that in the last analysis Marxism has only advanced industrialization without bringing about the longed-for humanization frustrates the young working people of today in the East, just as competition frustrates their counterparts in the West."[5] I doubt that we are ready, after only fifty years of much stress and strain, to assert anything about Marxism "in the last analysis." I also think that it distorts the evidence to affirm that in this half century Marxism has "only" advanced industrialization; its impact upon the status of women, upon the prevalence of literacy, upon the incidence of disease, and upon hundreds of millions of people as a vision and inspiration would surely make the use of the word "only" excessive.

If this is so, then one need not view dissatisfactions among some young people in the socialist lands as deriving out of Moltmann's reasons. They may more simply be explained on the basis of incomplete achievements, significant failings, remaining needs, and the immersion of these young people in a view that stresses the dynamic, abhors quiescence, glorifies revolutionary traditions and heroes, emphasizes responsibilities, highly estimates man, and has as its goal human emancipation. The persistence of discontent is a prerequisite for progress; to me the nearest thing to divinity is the inexhaustible and apparently ineradicable human capacity for feeling discontent. A civilization without discontent would be bovine, not human.

Moltmann does not see the Christian and the Marxist concepts of freedom as "simply opposing each other."[6] He rejects the view, stated in *Christianity Today* (October 27, 1967), that "Man's problem lies in his sins against the creator, not in domination by capitalistic forces." The miseries Christians seek to eliminate, he holds, are political, social, and natural, and insofar as that is true there is coincidence in the Christian and Marxist views.

Though the Marxist and Christian views of freedom are not contradictory, they also are not, writes Moltmann, identical. Christians hold, he declares, that man's miseries lie "not simply in their not yet realized possibilities, but even deeper in man's real impossibilities or his lost possibilities." We are here approaching what

Christians frankly call "mysteries," that is, areas that are not meant to be comprehended and are not subject to reason. Who knows the meaning of "real impossibilities"? How could one know their meaning if one simultaneously affirms that there exist "not yet realized possibilities"; perhaps realization of the latter would alter one's views of "real impossibilities"?

Man is "handed over to death, transitoriness, and nothingness," Moltmann believes, and for the Christian, therefore, freedom means "liberation from the curse of the evil deed through grace." We move here quite beyond the area of any possibility of dialogue with the Marxist, for we are utterly in the realm of "mystery"; this is not said in any spirit of hostility, let alone derision. It is said simply as a matter of fact: when the Christian in the course of a dialogue affirms as the essence of his conviction what is explicitly incomprehensible—that the very incomprehensibility is the content of the matter and the demonstration of the "reality"—one has moved not only away from dialogue but also from monologue, except insofar as prayer may be considered either one or the other.

Where such "mystery" is passionately believed and where it includes, for example, the ideas of life everlasting and the salvation of the soul as the center of life's meaning, one will have to provide great incentives indeed for the abandonment of such concepts. Parents who believe such ideas will resist or, at the very least, deeply resent efforts to organize life and society so as to threaten the beliefs making possible such prizes for their children. These considerations intensify the warnings uttered by Marx and Engels (and at times by Lenin) against anything smacking of religious persecution.

In the midst of his discussion of "mysteries," Moltmann asks the Marxist a familiar question; let us face it. ". . . one can ask why the Marxists seek their salvation on the earth and feel secure in earthly promises, if it may be likewise true that 'this' earth does not endure but will pass away."[7]

Marxists do not "seek salvation" on this earth or anywhere else. They seek justice, plenty, security, equality, peace, and creativity. Marxists do not feel "secure in earthly promises"; indeed, they do not feel secure at all. They feel anger and determination; security

43

is not for revolutionists. Nothing endures and everything passes away. A Marxist might agree with Teilhard de Chardin that

Man is not the center of the universe as once we thought in our simplicity, but something much more wonderful—the arrow pointing the way to the final unification of the world in terms of life. Man alone constitutes the last-born, the freshest, the most complicated, the most subtle of all the successive layers of life.[8]

Knowledge of this universe is severely limited and of other universes hardly begun. To see man in Teilhard's magnificent image in no way alters the basic concern of Marxism for the human condition, nor does it in any way deny man as the center of the earth. For the time that earth does endure and that man is here, let us work; there is enough to do and doing it is sufficient "salvation." Perhaps some of what is done will not "pass away"; in any case, one does what he can with the vision he has.

Finally, Moltmann asks more difficult questions of both Marxists and Christians. "All struggles for freedom," he writes, "are ambivalent." Hence Marxists face the question of how people, themselves alienated, may overcome alienation and not in the very struggle against it simultaneously create new alienations; for the Christian, how is it possible for those with sin to struggle against it without producing new sins?[9] Of both Marxists and Christians Moltmann asks: "How can the kingdom of nonviolent brotherhood be won without using violence?"

This is Dante's riddle, the man wrestling with the snake, winning, and slithering away. It is Brecht's lament to his fellow Communists; they who wanted kindness on earth had to be hard in order to triumph. Brecht does, however, confidently affirm that the art of kindness will be mastered. The peril of power and the curse of "success" exist; all history proves this. Marxism, struggling for power, tended to ignore problems connected with its possession; Seeking the overcoming of the "successful," it tended to minimize the corrosive quality of "success."

In its opposition to elitism, its insistence on mass participation and mass development, its drive toward equality, its commitment to the methods of science, its high estimate of man, and its purpose of human ennoblement, Marxism should have the capacity to overcome alienation. As for winning the kingdom of nonviolent brotherhood without violence, the greatest doubts exist. They exist not because Marxists are enamored of violence; on the contrary, they loathe it. But those possessed of power rest their possessions upon violence; they gained what they have with violence and they do not loathe it but make of it a cult to be worshiped and call it "patriotism" or "law and order."

The source of violence lies not with the dispossessed and the insulted; it lies with those who possess and insult, among whom mercy is the most foreign of attributes. Hence, whether or not violence is required depends basically on the balance of strength among the contending forces. If those with blood on their hands and rapacity in their hearts believe that they can use violence effectively to prevent their demise they will do so. Marxists are neither pacifists nor terrorists, and not being the former, resistance will be offered where violence appears; the issue will depend upon the relationship of forces at each moment.

It is worth observing that Moltmann assumes a common purpose in both Marxism and Christianity: the achievement without violence of the nonviolent brotherhood of man. He is affirming that with which this Marxist agrees. He is right in warning that "hard choices" confront us. Knowing this and also knowing the great resources available to those who contend for mutual goals will prevent enthusiasm's turning into resignation. I agree with his conclusion that precisely what is the nature of a "true humanity" and "a just order of the world" we do not yet know; I add that insofar as process is perpetual, we never will. But I feel no need to change a tittle in his closing remark: "What mankind should not be and which order of things is false we can know by consideration of the past and also by consideration of the future's possible development."[10]

2

Rarely has there appeared anywhere in literature—and rarely, indeed, in the United States—so remarkable a tribute to Marx as in Charles West's contribution to Ogletree's *Openings*. In "Act and Being in Christian and Marxist Perspective," West finds Marx to have been "a humanist in the full sense of that Renaissance and Enlightenment word." "Indeed," he continues, "his philosophy might be called humanism's richest autumn fruit, swollen with all the promises of the untrammeled human spirit, free from every authority to create its own future, and ripened by the sharp, cold frost of emancipated man's doubts and fears about the world he himself was making."[11] I would not want to add anything to that, but there is room for dialogue where West offers his views on Marx's and Lenin's ideas of knowledge and truth—basic, of course, to concepts of Act and Being.

West summarizes Marx's approach to knowledge and truth thus:

Knowledge is therefore not only relative to different points of view; it is distorted, an instrument of struggle. The claim to objective standards of truth or morals must always be hypocritical. The test of any truth is the source in the social struggle from which it comes and the practice to which it leads. "The question," wrote Marx in his second thesis on Feuerbach, "whether objective truth is an attribute of human thought is not a theoretical but a practical question. Man must prove the truth, i.e. the reality and power, the earthiness of his thinking in practice." His famous final thesis on Feuerbach, "Philosophers have interpreted the world in various ways; the point, however, is to change it," is not just a plea for social action. It is a statement of the condition of man and his capacity for knowledge at all.

The claim to objective standards of truth is not hypocritical in Marx or Marxism. Were the concept of objective truth abandoned, there would be neither point nor meaning to the Marxist concern about knowledge; but knowledge is a central concern for Marxism exactly because of the affirmation of the existence of objective truth. It is toward that objective truth that the accumulation of knowledge makes it possible to move. Were the existence of the truth denied, Marxism would become a theory of eternally receding

46

relativisms; it is not such a theory. It is a theory of historical and dialectical materialism, which means, among other things, that process and change are fundamental to its entire outlook, and that process and change are themselves part of the objective truth that, for Marxism, does indeed exist.

In its social vision, Marxism cuts the Gordian knot of objectivity —the dilemma presented by the unity between the thing observed and the observer—by affirming that it is the standpoint of the oppressed that offers the source making possible objective truth. Intense partisanship on the side of the oppressed is the way toward objectivity; this is the Marxist view. Of course, it may be in error, but whatever it is, it is not hypocritical in its affirmation of that objective reality and truth.

The second thesis on Feuerbach quoted not quite correctly by West is more than he makes of it: "a plea for social action" and "a statement of the condition of man and his capacity for knowledge at all." Central to it is the assertion of the unity of theory and practice; of the testing of theory by practice; of the need, if practice is to be effective, of having sound theory. It is also an affirmation of the idea that achieving the capacity to change the world indicates the effectiveness of the theory for such change, that is, of its grasp of reality. It seems to me, too, that Marx's thesis indicates that if one knew the real world one would want to change it; indeed, that a test of how well one knows it is how passionately one devotes oneself to those practices that will help change it.

The conclusion of Marx's second thesis on Feuerbach, which is not in West's quotation, and which is usually omitted by those who quote the famous and rhythmic line on understanding and changing, says: "The dispute over the reality or non-reality of thinking which is isolated from practice is a purely scholastic question." Note that the reality of thinking is not denied by Marx, *if* such thinking is not "isolated from practice."

The rhythmic line, too, as I indicated above, was not quoted precisely by West, and here it was not only a matter of omitting italics that appear in the original but also the inadvertent dropping of a word whose inclusion helps make clearer, I think, Marx's meaning. The last thesis on Feuerbach (1845) reads: "The philoso-

47

phers have only *interpreted* the world in various ways; the point
however is to *change* it." Replacing the word "only" before *"interpreted"* helps to preserve Marx's emphasis on the inadequacy of
mere contemplation—without participation—if one seeks comprehension.

Having erroneously declared that Marx denied objective truth,
West states that Lenin affirmed, "unlike Marx, [that] there was no
doubt that Marxist theory itself was the absolute truth."[12] As sub-
stantiation, he offers the following from Lenin: "you cannot eliminate even one basic assumption, one substantial part of this
philosophy of Marxism (it is as if it were a solid block of steel)
without abandoning objective truth, without falling into the arms
of bourgeois reactionary falsehood."[13] From this West concludes
that integral to the Leninist view (distortion) of Marxism is a rigid,
rote-like conception, appropriate to the image of a "block of steel."
Here, again, dialogue is indicated.

In the quotation offered, attention should be given to the fact that
Lenin is talking about the "elimination" of "basic assumptions" as
leading to the vitiation of objective truth (note, by the way, Lenin's
assumption of its existence). Such a view follows naturally if one
holds—and Marxists do—that the Marxist view represents a world
outlook that is, in fact, scientific. This means that it is an approxi-
mation; it means that Marxism assumes the necessity for correction
of error since that is the way science advances; and it means the
existence of change, growth, and decay, the coming into being and
the disappearance, the whole reality of process and of dynamism
that is the very heart of matter itself.

Hence, to Marxism and to Lenin, rigidity guarantees error;
dogma is the opposite of science. This does not mean, of course,
that in the name of Marxism persons may not behave with rigidity
and be guilty of dogmatism; rigidity among scientists as such and
the adoption of dogmatic approaches by them also are not unknown
failings, but these faults do not negate science, though they certainly have not assisted its progress.

In the preface to the very work from which West quotes, Lenin
refers to "some antiquated views of Marx," particularly on "some
historical questions." Engels, in *Anti-Dühring*, noting "how young

48

the whole of human history is," went on to observe, therefore, "how ridiculous it would be to attempt to ascribe any absolute validity to our present view." Again, in *Our Program* (1899), Lenin states: "To defend a theory of this kind [Marxism] of the truth of which one is completely convinced, against unfounded attacks and against attempts to debase it, does not mean being an enemy of criticism in general." "We by no means," Lenin continued, "regard the theory of Marxism as perfect and inviolable; on the contrary, we are convinced that this theory has only laid the foundation stones of that science on which the socialists must continue to build in every direction, unless they wish to be left behind by life."[14]

This matter is of the greatest importance not only in a philosophic sense but also in terms of the effort of Ogletree's book. If one is persuaded, as West writes, that a Marxist-Leninist believes that he already possesses "the absolute truth," all dialogue—or, at least, serious discussion—is foreclosed. The spirit and content of this outlook is, rather, that expressed by the superb Communist, Antonio Gramsci, while he was in one of Mussolini's prisons:

The most advanced thinker is he who understands that his adversary may express a truth which should be incorporated in his own ideas, even if in a minor way. To understand and evaluate realistically the positions and reasons of one's adversary (and sometimes the adversary is the entire thought of the past) means to have freed oneself from the prison of ideologies, in the sense of blind fanaticism.

3

Paul Lehmann, professor of theology at Union Theological Seminary in New York, in "Christian Theology in a World in Revolution," takes a very positive view of Marxism-Leninism in terms of its persistent and intense appeal, but a distinctly dismal view in terms of its practice. Quite apart from this distinction to which one cannot agree, Lehmann writes:

... while we are living in a post-Christian world, we are not living in a post-Marxian one. Marxism-Leninism is still the bearer of the revolutionary ferment of our time. It is the bearer of this ferment in the sense that despite the stresses and strains of power, of heresy and schism within the communist movement, the Marxist-Leninist account of the impact of power upon social change and of social change upon power is still the point from which to take our bearings in the revolutionary situation in which we live.[15]

While I am less certain than Lehmann that we are indeed "living in a post-Christian world," I am encouraged to find him so positive in his evaluation of the existing appeal of Marxism-Leninism. There are, however, certain views of that theory which Lehmann expresses that I find dubious; it is possible that here we have some explanation for his dismal evaluation of it in practice. On both points, we wish to enter the dialogue again.

Lehmann seems to hold the view that a "people's revolution" meant, to Marx, a peaceful revolution and that the exclusion of the latter makes impossible the former. Thus, referring to the impact that the Commune had upon both Marx and Engels—leading them, as I noted earlier, to remark that their *Manifesto* was "especially" outdated insofar as it did not see the necessity to smash the bourgeois state apparatus in order to move towards socialism—Lehmann writes that Marx distinguished England from the European continent by affirming that in the former "a minimal bureaucracy and the absence of a militarist clique seemed to make for the possibility even of a people's revolution."[16]

The point here—as made by Marx and, drawing upon him, by Lenin—is not that in England, unlike the Continent, the possibility of a people's revolution existed, but rather that in England (and in the United States) for the reasons given, such a revolution was possible "*without* the preliminary condition," as Lenin wrote and italicized in *State and Revolution* (Chapter III) of smashing the existing state apparatus. This means, in effect, that the possibility of the peaceful transition to socialism was seen by Marx in the 1870s insofar as England, the United States, and Holland were concerned; and that given such transition, he saw different requirements facing revolutionists in terms of both the character and the function of the state. Lenin agreed with Marx on this; but nothing here involved in the remotest degree an affirmation that a "people's revolution" was possible under conditions of peaceful transition and impossible under other conditions.[17]

Another significant limitation in Lehmann's presentation of the Marxist-Leninist view of the socialist revolution is his failure to note that it emphasized the distinction between the lower and the higher stages of society resulting from that revolution, that is, between socialism and communism. Certainly, as Lehmann writes Marxism-Leninism couples equality with freedom[18]; but neither Marx nor Lenin held that equality and freedom would exist during the transition period from capitalism to communism. On the contrary, both emphasized that in the transition period equality and actual freedom would be significantly enhanced for the majority of people, but neither would be fully achieved for any, and that weighty limitations would exist in both areas for the majority of the population, let alone for the minority whose dominant position in the former society had been overthrown.

Marx and Lenin based these conclusions simply on the *internal* difficulties and antagonisms that the socialist revolution would face; Lenin lived long enough to see how much substance would be added to them because of *external* hostilities and obstacles. One would think that since Lehmann, writing more than forty years after Lenin's death, knows of the twenty-five million killed in the Soviet Union in the Second World War, he would pay some attention to this problem of transition from socialism to communism before dismissing Lenin's revolution as a "failure."

Lehmann quotes part of a paragraph from Lenin's *State and Revolution* where he sees democracy as meaning equality, and real democracy as requiring the elimination of classes. He quotes, too, the portion in which Lenin affirms the need of so developing the socioeconomic order that the realization of "from each according to his ability, to each according to his needs" would become actual, as well as Lenin's remark that through what stages and exactly by what practical measures "humanity will proceed to this supreme aim—we do not and cannot know." This paragraph has a concluding sentence, not quoted by Lehmann, that makes Lenin's basic point, namely, the transitional character of socialism, the fact that it is not fixed; the sentence is also relevant to Charles West's tendency to present socialism, in the Marxist view, as static. Lenin, after writing that "we do not and cannot know," went on to affirm:

But it is important to realize how infinitely mendacious is the ordinary bourgeois conception of socialism as something lifeless, rigid, fixed, once and for all, whereas in reality *only* socialism will be the beginning of a rapid, genuine, truly mass forward movement, embracing first the *majority* and then the whole of the population, in all spheres of public and private life. (Lenin's italics.)

Lehmann supports his position by calling upon the considerable authority of Barrington Moore, Jr., from whose *Soviet Politics: The Dilemma of Power* he quotes as follows:

Lenin and his followers set out to achieve for humanity the goals of freedom and equality by means of an organization that denied these same principles. It was anticipated that denial would be temporary and that the fruits of victory would bring the goals desired. Instead, discipline, authority, and inequality had to be intensified after victory.[19]

I would agree with almost nothing in this passage, central to both Lehmann and Moore. Marxist-Leninists (Communists) certainly have as a goal, at least in their own minds, freedom and equality, but they do not set out to realize this goal by means of an organization denying such principles. The goal of freedom and equality is something to be reached, Communists think, only after the overthrow of capitalism, the experience of socialism, and the development out of that experience of a communist society. Hence, it is simply absurd to write that Communists, while laboring to transform capitalism, create an organization denying goals to be achieved only after the transition from socialism to communism.

The organization Marxist-Leninists created for the achievement of the transformation of capitalist society was a Communist party; that Party, as conceived by Lenin, was one of like-minded people who sought to assist in that transformation. Membership was voluntary and mutually agreed upon; majority sentiment was decisive but unanimity was sought; argument was encouraged, self-criticism demanded, solidarity required, and policy was tested and retested in practice.

With the achievement of state power, Marx affirmed and Lenin

52

emphasized that the nature of the state altered from one that hitherto had been an instrument to enforce the will of a ruling class based upon possession of the means of production to a ruling class —working people and allies—whose purpose was the elimination of such possession and the institution of socialist relations of production. This "dictatorship of the proletariat" was not an organization that denied the principles of freedom and equality partially for the reasons just offered in terms of the party. But basically, it was not such an organization because it was fully understood by Marx and Lenin and emphasized by both that there would be a prolonged period marking the transition from full capitalist power to full worker power, politically, and from a basically capitalist form of economy to a basically socialist form, and that there would then be another period of transition—the socialist form having been achieved—from socialism to communism. It was not then a matter of "anticipating that denial would be temporary"; it was, first of all, the reality of a marked extension of equality and freedom for most of the population—not yet full equality or freedom for any, but considerable enhancement of the perquisites of both for many. It also was "anticipated" that this effort would provoke intense opposition and that such opposition had to be withstood at the cost of great discipline, sacrifice, and struggle.

With the transformation of the state from one dominated by the bourgeoisie and its allies to one dominated by working people and their allies, "discipline and authority" certainly "had to be intensified," and neither Moore nor Lehmann—nor anyone else—has proposed an alternative (except to surrender). Inequality was not intensified in revolutionary Russia, vis-à-vis the Russia that preceded it, quite the contrary; but in the movement from the one to the other discipline and authority were intensified; and if they had not been, the Revolution would have collapsed in about the time set for that eventuality by the *New York Times* and President Wilson.

Moore called what he was expounding in the quoted paragraph a "double paradox," and Lehmann goes on from there to remark that "The paradox, of course, spells historical and revolutionary failure." Lehmann feels that "Each in its own way, Marxism and

Christianity have drawn a blank exactly at the point at which the problem of power shatters the power of revolution to achieve humanization."[20] I do think that problems of power, the temptations of power, and questions of how power is exercised have been minimized in the literature of Marxism,[21] but I do not think such problems are insoluble nor do I agree that they have produced "failure" in any objective and historically oriented evaluation of the Bolshevik Revolution and later transitions to socialism elsewhere. To write off as "failures" one movement that covers twenty centuries and another that—insofar as power is concerned—covers less than six decades would appear to show something approaching impatience, if not malice, toward the second.

Nowhere in Lehmann's estimate of Lenin's "failure" is there the slightest consideration of what it was with which he began: a Russia backward to begin with and shattered after almost four years of war; a Russia whose European population was sixty-five per cent and its Asian population ninety-five per cent illiterate; a Russia whose women were infinitely subordinated; a Russia whose church was Byzantine and whose unity of church and state had been complete; a Russia that had been the prison-house of nationalities and the center of virulent, institutionalized racism and anti-Semitism. So much for the barest sketch of the internal reality that must be weighed with great care—not to say compassion—before labeling the Leninist effort as "a failure, of course."

Omitted, too, from the Lehmann evaluation is any reflection of the realities of what Lenin's Russia faced (and faces) in terms of external threats and hostilities. It is not necessary to spell out the details from the White Guard assaults to the Allied interventions to Hitler's mercies and Dulles' friendship, but it is wrong to evaluate the historic meaning of the Bolshevik Revolution and the state it brought into being and in doing so to *ignore* this past—and this present.

Something of a response to Lehmann is made in the very volume to which he contributed. Sidney Lens, in "The Changing Character of Communism," notes that "To contain communism and to roll it back, our own country has spent $900,000,000,000 on its military establishment since the end of the war."[22] (One may now make the total a round trillion dollars.) Do such expenditures by a state for such purposes require a response from the USSR? And does such a response—political, social, and psychological as well as economic-military—have any impact upon the realities of life in the Soviet Union? It is not possible to controvert Lens's remark:

> Our military and political leaders have built hundreds of military bases around the world to encircle the Communist nations, hold them in check for the moment, until—hopefully—the moment arrives when communism can be rolled back and destroyed. Our forty thousand megatons of hydrogen bombs . . .; our chemical, bacterial, and radiological weapons; our many military treaties; our intervention in Vietnam, Thailand, the Dominican Republic, and elsewhere, are all part of this strategy.[23]

Nor is it possible to doubt the truth of Lens's view that

> If there is one thing in the character of communism that stands out, it is that its forms are vitally affected by international relationships and international pressures. We do not know what type of communism would have emerged if the Allies had not decided to send fourteen armies to the Soviet Union in 1918, or if they had not underwritten the military efforts of the counter-revolutionary White Guards.[24]

Let me add—since Lens does not—that the appearance of fascism in Europe, and especially its gaining power in Germany, similarly had a profound effect upon developments within the USSR and upon the thinking of all Communists; so, too, did World War II, with its cost in human and economic terms.

The realities of the inheritance of the Bolsheviks and the external threats to the USSR—and other socialist states—are not recalled here in any defensive way because, despite all the crimes, failures, and setbacks, the actual accomplishments of the USSR and other socialist nations are extraordinary. That these were registered despite what was faced—in particular, despite the holocaust of World War II—is explicable only, I believe, in terms of the irresistible might based upon socialist foundations.

The socialist world, Lens writes, "has far stronger economies, it provides far better for its people than we have been led to believe, and it has greater self-confidence." On the basis of his study and personal and repeated examinations, Lens concludes that "the

Communist world is here to stay." He adds:

> It will be modified, altered, remolded toward greater economic and political democracy, but it wouldn't be overthrown either from within or from without. The Communist regimes are not as unpopular with their people as our public information officers pretend. It is worth noting that while every single adult in North Vietnam has a gun in his hand, Ho Chi Minh can walk amongst them with less fear of assassination than President Johnson or the late President Kennedy. Or, that while a half million Cubans are armed with weapons—the largest militia in the Western Hemisphere—no effort has been made by them to topple the Castro government, and so far as I know there has been no killing of an important Cuban leader, though they circulate often amongst the male and female militia.[25]

When the Socialist states are evaluated in terms of their own pasts—that is, the Bulgaria of King Boris, the Rumania of Queen Marie, the Cuba of Batista, and so on—there is no question whatsoever that in every category of concern to one who desires humanization such as child care, sufficient food, general health, levels of education, hours and conditions of labor, possibilities of rest and leisure, realities of cultural participation and opportunities, status of women and formerly oppressed peoples, participation in political and social matters, the verdict spells historical and revolutionary success.

If the next five decades see as the portion of Marxism-Leninism the "failures" of the preceding five, it is likely that the world in 2020 A.D. will be devoid of both colonialism and capitalism and will be organized in socialist-communist ways.

Chapter Four

Love and the Transcendental

If religion were defined in the phrase of Ralph Barton Perry—
"man's profoundest solicitude about the things he counts most
valuable"[1]—there would surely be no point in pressing for a dialogue between Marxism and religion; one would discuss only what
"he counts most valuable." Dean James W. Culliton of Notre Dame
defined religion as "the concept that man is different from other
animals and therefore seems to have moral values"[2]; in this case,
too, the Marxist individual and the religious one would not have
significant areas of difference.

With the secularization of religion and with the common omis-
sion of God in what is offered as religion today, one can understand
the efforts made at the shorthand definitions suggested above. The
word itself has been derived from two similar Latin words: *religere*,
to execute painstakingly by means of repeated effort, and *religare*,
to bind together, as a "bond of piety." Both concepts are clearly
part of religion, but fundamental is "religion as the complex of
man's interrelations with superhuman powers," with "magic" being
"more or less the corner stone of every historical religion," and
with the experiences defined as peculiarly religious being "essentially ecstatic in character."[3]

Whatever may be the religion's formal definition, however, one

57

element is never absent, no matter how secularized or demytholo-
gized religion has become. This is a note of high moral concern, of
ethical emphasis, of something transcendental; from this perspective religious man speaks of man as "different from other animals"
and as witness to and the crowning glory of God (or whatever term
is desired).

This argument from the transcendental is made quite graphically
—if somewhat surprisingly, given his occupation—by O. H. Ohmann, writing while assistant to the president of the Standard Oil
Corporation of Ohio. Ohman finds that the basic difference between what he calls Communism, as in the USSR, and "our system"
is not in productivity, where both do well, or in developing loyalties
among their respective populations, in which, again, he says, both
do well. "No, the real difference is in the philosophy about people.
. . . Are all standards of conduct man-made and relative, or absolute
and eternal? Is man a meaningless happenstance of protoplasm, or
is he a divine creation with a purpose, with potential for improvement, and with a special destiny in the over-all scheme of things?"
As something of a nonsequitor, Ohmann concludes that it was "The
absence of these values [that] permitted the Nazis to 'process'
people through the gas chambers . . .," a nonsequitor because if
there were two conditions not characteristic of Nazis, these were
being Russians and being Communists.[4]

Still, Ohmann's crudeness perhaps sharpens the point; namely,
there exist but two alternative views of man: "a meaningless happenstance of protoplasm" or "a divine creation"; and those, like
Communists, who believe the first, necessarily end up as moral
idiots. Communists, then, are all of stomach and believe everyone
else is, too; they have no feeling for the finer things of life, to say
nothing of an afterlife; they devalue the individual in their fanatical
concern with the collective; and the latter concern derives from
their concept of humans as robots to be manipulated—for purposes
of power or domination, or (being moral idiots), for purposes of the
Devil.

The Reverend Johannes Hamel, writing of *A Christian in East
Germany*, tells of a conversation he had with a Communist, who
had demanded of him: "How can God be real, if He is not material.

Only material is real!" The reply came, pointing out to the Communist—characteristically, he had never thought of this himself—that love and trust existed between him and his wife and that this was "real" though it was not "material." This led him at once to agree "that his concept of reality didn't suffice to explain human beings and their relation to each other." It was possible, then, for Hamel to take another step: "I showed him then that the whole of Marxism gives no answer to the question, what the death of a human being really is, and that therefore it cannot answer the question what a man is, because we exist only as men who die. Here lurks the real evil in our lives, for which Marxism offers no help."

Objections such as that offered by the Reverend Mr. Hamel make a caricature of Marxism, of course; they identify Marxism with the crudest kind of vulgar materialism and hand over to what is called "religion" sole concern with questions of morals, ethics, comp sion, mercy, and purpose of life. In a similar manner, the distinguished historian of science, George Sarton, wrote of "three quests" known to human beings: "for goodness and justice (that is religion), for beauty (that is art), for truth (that is science)."[5] His compartmentalization falsifies each, but—to the point at the moment—with such a definition of religion, obviously one who is irreligious is a monster. Sarton spares the reader this, perhaps, in his remark that man "invented God," but the weight of his definition, as of the others cited above, is to identify religion with virtue and irreligion with vice. This is especially consequential in the United States, whose population is, as polls have repeatedly shown, perhaps the most religious of all; indeed, Marx himself noted this characteristic prior to the Civil War, and commented that part of the public definition of an honest American was religious affiliation.[6]

Today, happily, it is possible to begin one's reply to this characteristic misrepresentation of Marxism as a kind of crass materialism by quoting a Roman Catholic priest, the secretary to the Spanish episcopacy, Father Guerva Banyres. He writes:

Marxism is not a vulgar form of materialism. It is atheistic because atheism is an integral part of its world outlook. It believes in the need for and the adequacy of material reality, while religion and idealism thrust man beyond its confines, alienate him and hamper his liberation. This atheism is, therefore, not a denial, but an expression of humanism which has its own eschatology. It is necessary that we understood that denial of the transcendental as far as Marxists are concerned is not a fault but a virtue since it enables man to rediscover himself.[7]

Human beings make themselves and God, too; the making of God reflects humanity's alienation in a world and a society still unknown and significantly defective. For Marxism, not only is it true that nothing human is alien; it is also true that nothing higher than humanity exists. It is to overcome, as Marx said, all of humanity's limitations, all of its humiliations, all indignities and inadequacies that Marxism exists. No intermediary or intercessor is required; if one were required it would dethrone humanity, demean man, and make impossible *his own* liberation. Anything other than his own is not liberation but mysticism. His own liberation is desired, by himself and for himself and here on earth. For this God is more than an irrelevancy; He is an obstacle.

Among the decisive points of distinction between Marxism and earlier forms of materialism is that Marxism is based on man's creativity, man's activity, man's practice. This is the essential point in each of Marx's eleven *Theses on Feuerbach*. To summarize them: (1) "The chief defect in all hitherto existing materialism" lay in its depiction of reality in the form only of object, "or of *contemplation*" rather than as "human sensuous activity, practice." Practice appeared only in idealism, but appeared there necessarily in an aborted, divorced form. Marx's point is the necessity of combining object and subject, which conveys the basic consequence of revolutionary " 'practical-critical' activity." It follows (2) that the reality or nonreality of thinking cannot be resolved if it is "isolated from practice," for if it is, it becomes "a purely *scholastic* question."

Hence, too, follows the limitation within the conventional materialist view (such as Robert Owen's) that men are products of circumstances and of upbringing; this view neglects the facts (3) that "it is men that change circumstances and that the educator himself needs educating." There is and must be a "coincidence of the changing of circumstances and of human activity," and this can be understood only as *"revolutionizing practice."* One may add here that not only do men (and women) make circumstances and circumstances make men (and women), but also that they—men and women—are themselves part of the "circumstances"; the interpenetration is complete and is of the essence of the whole process and the whole reality.

In the fourth thesis, Marx turns directly to "the fact of religious self-alienation." He pays tribute to Feuerbach for demonstrating "the dissolution of the religious world into its secular basis," but then adds the crucial Marxist criticism that having done this "the chief thing still remains to be done," that is, to comprehend the source of such self-alienation in the "secular basis." This basis must be comprehended and the contradiction in it which induces the alienation must be overcome, "revolutionized in practice."

The remainder of the *Theses* then develop the idea that contemplation removed from *"practical,* human-sensuous activity" is deficient; that thinking of human beings separated from society is erroneous abstracting. The latter view makes it possible to ignore the fact that religiosity itself is "a *social product."* And social life itself "is essentially *practical";* mysticism is resolved in such practice and in the comprehension of that practice. Hence a materialism that is only contemplative will not work, and among its inadequacies is its failure to possess "the standpoint" of the *"human* society, or socialized humanity." All this is the prelude to the crashing Thesis IX already quoted: "The philosophers have only *interpreted* the world, in various ways; the point, however, is to *change* it."

How one can still find persistence in the kind of distortions offered in the Rev. Mr. Hamels's words almost passes comprehension, except when one bears in mind Marx's own insistence upon ideology as a *social* and *practical* product.

The transcendental connotes the mystical; at the heart of religion is this insistence upon mystery. Indeed, classically, it was the very fact of alleged incomprehensibility that was the "proof" of religion. In the Book of Job the whole point is that man knows nothing and can know nothing and to acknowledge this is the limit open to man's pitiful "wisdom." Out of the whirlwind, in the heart of Job (28:1–28), God makes it clear that man's faith comes not from knowing, not from reward, not from promise, and not from retribution; it comes from nothing at all except faith in Him and to be real it must surpass understanding.

> But wisdom, where shall it be found?
> And where is the place of understanding?
> No mortal knoweth the pathway to it;
> Neither is it found in the land of the living.
>   . . .
> And unto man He said:
> "Behold, the fear of the Lord, that is wisdom;
> And to depart from evil is understanding."

To make His point, God makes a pact with Satan and gives him control over Job's life. Afflictions without end fall upon Job: his children die, his servants die, his cattle die, his wealth vanishes, his body putrifies, and his wife deserts him insofar as she pleads with him to yield and to curse God as the Devil urges (always it is the woman who is weak and who yields). But Job's faith endures, though the worst befalls—test me, test me—this faith persists and that is God's victory!

As Hayim Greenberg wrote in 1940: "Religious man . . . must learn from Job to believe without understanding, to trust without explanations."[8] Or, more recently, from Marvin H. Pope's introduction to Job in *The Anchor Bible:*

> But how can a man put his faith in such a One who is the slayer of all? Faith in Him is not achieved without moral struggle and spiritual agony. The foundation of such a faith has to be laid in utter despair of reliance on any or all lesser causes and in resignation which has faced and accepted the worst and the best life can offer. Before this One no man is clean. To Him all human righteousness is as filthy rags. The transition from fear and hatred to trust and even love of this One—from God the Enemy to God the Friend and Companion—is the pilgrimage of every man of faith. Job's journey from despair to faith is the way each mortal must go.[9]

If one is to take the Gospel as written by Mark and Matthew (rather than by Luke and John), the last words of God's Son on the cross were: "My God, my God, why hast thou forsaken me?" This would seem to indicate that he, unlike Job, went not from despair to faith but from faith to despair. Mystery resolves this, too, as Frederick Buechner has written, "all attempts to explain it in terms of the divine scheme of things are in the last analysis only words, just words." But, he adds, beyond this is faith, "that for Jesus, and for countless generations through Jesus, not even despair could prevent the rising up of new hope, new life, new openness to the love that holds the very stars in their courses."[10] If such faith leads to moving forward in this world rather than resting supine in hopes of redemption in another, as so many of the most modern theologians suggest, the Marxist would not find the inspiration persuasive but would not on that account dismiss it.

On the other hand, the man whose very name symbolizes modern science, Einstein, and who himself was a Socialist, affirmed his belief in the mystical and, in that sense, declared himself profoundly religious. In his words:

The most beautiful emotion we can experience is the mystical. It is the true sower of all true art and science. He to whom this emotion is a stranger, who can no longer wonder and stand rapt in awe, is as good as dead. To know that what is impenetrable to us really exists, manifesting itself as the highest wisdom and the most radiant beauty, which our dull faculties can comprehend only in their most primitive forms—this knowledge, this feeling, is at the center of true religiousness. In this sense, and in this sense only, I belong to the ranks of devoutly religious men.[11]

Much of Einstein's feeling would be embraced by a Marxist, but not all of it. The capacity for wonder and even awe cannot be absent from a revolutionary, particularly if he has experienced solidarity and comradeship in struggle (and what revolutionary hasn't?). But certainty of the existence of that which cannot be penetrated (whatever that may be) and this sense of certainty as "highest wisdom" —no, I fear a Marxist would have to reject this, for he finds it necessary to reject mystery in general. This has nothing to do with the rejection of that which inspires awe or with a deep spirituality, a profound passion without which one may have a fanatic but not a revolutionist.

The most beautiful emotion we can experience is not mystical; it is love, it is the sense of human solidarity, of selflessness through

63

which the self is found. It is the feeling you have in combat, any kind of real combat, that cements you with those struggling with you; and it is the feeling you have towards one with whom you share life, with all its doubts and agonies and glories. If this is religious, so be it. It is what suffuses the greatest writing, including that produced by such Communists as Neruda, O'Casey, Gorky, Aragon, Fuchik, Guillen, Seghers, MacDiarmid, and Brecht.

In a recent issue of the French Communist journal, *La Nouvelle Critique*, Michel Verret writes "On Love and Marxism," and perhaps an American will be pardoned if, when writing of love, he borrows heavily from one who is French. Verret writes that "It is not love that he [the Marxist] refuses. It is phrases about love." And he goes on: "To hold this an offense against love, we would have to suppose that love cannot do without phrases. But when does love speak? When it does not yet know, or when it has forgotten, how to help. . . . Otherwise, love does not talk. It helps."[12]

On the other hand, love itself is not enough if one is to accomplish the assistance; it may motivate the undertaking but it will not assure the result. Thus Verret says: "If children are without milk and books, love will not fill their hunger. They need love, plus milk and books." Love can help motivate the effort to change the world, but to actually change it takes not love alone but consciousness and direction and struggle and power.

Verret says that this concentration upon action and change may develop hardness, and while to be hard is necessary, it is possible —as Brecht also warned—to be too hard, even though one is trying to make a world in which kindness is possible. "We are not always equal to our love," writes Verret. "Maybe hardness deforms it," and alas, the examples of such deformities are not few. But where the world is terribly hard, to refrain from being hard may be to become weak. And for the Communist, as Verret says, there is "the hardness of him who bears too much hatred (in the eyes of many, an injury done to a Communist is not an injury—but for the Communist, it is one)." And he enumerates instances of hardness briefly, as "Hardness that must face superhuman tasks: to survive at Buchenwald, to die at Stalingrad." I would add and amend: not only to survive but also to rebel at Buchenwald as the prisoners did, led

by the German Communist, Walter Bartel, and not to die at Stalingrad but to live, and to triumph. Hardness is needed, but love, too
—love as fierce as the ovens and the bombs.

From Job and from Christ's final lament—from much of religion
—the Marxist may learn if he did not already know, or if in his haste
he had forgotten, that living is suffering, too, and that much suffering is personal. There are a million problems besetting people that
arise quite apart from politics (certainly politics in any narrow
sense): a retarded child, an accidental death. Much may be done
socially even for these, but by no means everything, and in that
sense, there remains a pain to be nursed alone or with a very few.
A rational social order certainly is not the whole of happiness, but
it does constitute a prerequisite therefor. Verret adds the thought,
which will not be new to those steeped in the best of religious
thought, but may be somewhat startling to those who have sum-
marily rejected or never encountered such thought: "that progress
is not always innocent, and that it can even erect new crosses."

From sharing God the deeply religious gather love; many among
them feel that those of us who do not share Him are therefore shorn
of love, and in that sense not fully human. Still, if we do not share
God, we may share mankind; will there then not be love enough?

In arguing Marxism's rejection of mystery and mysticism, I know
that the Thomist scholar, Gustav A. Wetter, has insisted:

> Despite its campaign against any sort of "mysticism," dialectical materi-
> alism, with its doctrine of "contradictions" in the world, has restored to
> its adherents a feeling for the paradox and mystery of the world and has
> thereby prepared the ground for the revival of a truly philosophical "sense
> of wonder." ... Dialectical materialism, despite its verbal hostility to all
> forms of "mysticism," is nevertheless endued at bottom with a certain
> "mystical" vein.[13]

But Father Wetter merely asserts the presence of this vein and
does not assist his argument by using "paradox" interchangeably
with "mystery." Paradoxes abound, but they do not have mysteri-
ous essences. Where certain mystics—such as Meister Eckhart and
Jakob Boehme—tended, as John Lewis wrote over thirty years ago,
to dissolve "the idea of a separate transcendent Deity into the

conception of the potentiality of being," and that Marxism "never attempts to reduce spirit to matter, but, on the contrary, declares that spiritual activities are the highest function of matter,"[14] these mystics were expressing difficulties with the conventional and orthodox views of God. Their expressions of such difficulties in no way suggest mysticism in Marxism!

Lately, in attempting to further the argument as to Marxism's "inherent mysticism," Alfred Stiernotte has suggested that perhaps it is "the whole mystical and cosmic theology" of Teilhard de Chardin that has made such Marxists as Joseph Needham (and Roger Garaudy, one may add) take so favorable a view of Teilhard's work.[15] But the Marxists who have written about Teilhard have made clear—and let me add to their number—that his great attraction is his concept of evolution and progress, of contradiction and antagonism, of commitment to a God who is in front and leading forward rather than to one who is above and urging resignation.[16] The obvious coincidences here with elements in Marxism made Teilhard view it with considerable favor, and helped to account for the intense degree of official disfavor the Church measured out to him. All this is hardly a convincing argument for the mysticism of Marxism, though it argues the attractiveness of Marxism for some who still view themselves as religious mystics.

Chapter Five

Ethics and Humanity

The works of Marx, Engels, Lenin, and many other Marxist writers contain attacks upon moralizing; these have often been confused with attacks upon morality. One may find in the three giants explicit and repeated denunciations of "love," "justice," "Rights," "higher ideals," and "true love of humanity." This has induced some writers—including some who insist they are Marxists—to depict Marxism as the foe of morality or even as amoral.

Nothing could be more false; nothing distorts Marxism more than to strip it of its ethical commitment. If and when this is done one has a gross falsification; if it is done in the name of Marxism one has a robotized caricature of the real outlook that may develop the characteristics and the appetites of Frankenstein's monster.

The reality here is substantially the same as that offered by Michel Verret in his essay on love and Marxism. Vernon Venable has an excellent explanation for this particular strain of polemics in the classical Marxist writings. "The reason," he wrote, ". . . was not, in fact, that Marx and Engels were deficient in moral consciousness, but on the contrary, as is evident when one reads the texts with any care and searchingness, that they had too much of it to tolerate the hypocrisy or stupidity of lip service."[1]

The horrors of industrial capitalism in the nineteenth century had spawned a host of reformers—such as Proudhon, Fourier, Owen, and Dühring—with more or less Utopian outlooks that, Marx and Engels felt, were inadequate when not downright misleading. They had in common a superabundance of idealistic phraseology and a minimum of fundamental social analysis, effective programs, or comprehension of the role and task of the working class. Hence Marx and Engels polemized against them; these polemics included denunciations of appeals to ethical and moral goals detached from time, place, circumstance, and class, and therefore verging into sheer cant.

"It was this," Venable rightly pointed out, "not ethics, moral responsibility, genuinely humanist equlitarianism or real justice that Marx and Engels were attacking in their attacks upon ethical idealism." This is not unlike Lenin's attacks upon such reformers as the "god-builders" in pre-1917 Russia, to which attention was called earlier.

No doubt the Marxist rejection of moral absolutes evokes the kind of criticism indicated in John Middleton Murry's remark that "The bias of Marxism is toward the elimination of the moral and religious processes from history."[2] Quite apart from Murry's joining of the moral and the religious—related to my earlier remark that theists often think of atheists as moral idiots—his remark errs, too, because Marxism, far from seeking to eliminate the moral from the processes of history, feels that without considering historical process it is not possible to comprehend morals. Here, for example, is Engels on this subject:

> The conceptions of good and bad have varied so much from nation to nation and from age to age that they have often been in direct contradiction to each other. But all the same, someone may object, good is not bad and bad is not good. ... But the matter cannot so simply be disposed of. ... What morality is preached to us today? There is first Christian-feudal morality, inherited from past periods of faith; and this again has two main subdivisions, Catholic and Protestant moralities, each of which in turn has no lack of further subdivisions. ... Alongside of these we find the modern bourgeois morality and with it too the proletarian morality of the future,

so that in the most advanced European countries alone the past, present and future provide three great groups of moral theories which are in force simultaneously and alongside of each other.[3]

Where different social orders have similar institutions—such as the existence of private property—all may have similar moral (and legal) injunctions, as "thou shalt not steal." But these have significant variations in fact. For example, shall a slave steal? If he does steal, is he stealing when he takes from his master? The slaves themselves in the United States thought not; their morality taught them that to steal was to take that which another slave possessed, but to take from the master was not wrong but right, since, as the slaves said: "We produce all and therefore *should* have all." And what of the mother who steals to feed a hungry child? Is not the immorality in the society permitting a child to go hungry and not in the mother so acting?

And does not this society institutionalize stealing, that is, looting, as by cartels and monopolists in so-called developed countries working their wills upon so-called underdeveloped countries (which are not so much underdeveloped as overexploited and therefore "underdeveloped"); or in prices charged and credit rates imposed within ghetto areas, all of which is "legal" and normal. Looting appears in the ghetto only when its residents take furniture and food and neglect to pay these "special" prices for especially poor merchandise.

And "thou shalt not kill"—unless it is Vietnamese! Unless it is through malnutrition. Unless it is through foul housing, with its resultant lead poisoning of infants and its war of rats versus babies —and its high rents![4] Unless it is through being poor and so having a death rate two or three or five times higher than those who are rich.

More specifically, surely one should not enter another's bedroom and smash in the skull of one asleep there? But suppose the one asleep is Joseph Travis and the one coming in through the light of the moon is Nat Turner? One might add here that the concept of retribution itself—personal and historic—does seem never to have been absent from human history in some form. And historic retribution is by no means confined to Judaeo-Christian thought; it appears in Marx in quite a literal form. Thus, for example, writing on "The Indian Revolt" for the *New York Daily Tribune* (September 16, 1857), Marx declared: "There is something in human history like retribution; and it is a rule of historical retribution that its instrument be forged not by the offended, but by the offender himself."[5]

In their concern for the historical and the social, at times Marx and Engels wrote not only in a manner that made possible the kinds of distortions we have seen relating to love and morals but also to such questions as slavery and colonialism. There seems at times to be so great a concentration upon the historical process that the individuals involved are lost or disregarded; as applied to the Marxist projection of the future, a similar kind of misreading—and similar kinds of erroneous emphases, too—produce the charge of impersonality, of harshness, of ignoring the means to accomplish the ends, and so on.

In an important study, Horace Davis has remarked that

by quoting passages from the writings of Marx and Engels out of context, it has been possible for one school of writers to make them out as apologists for slavery and imperialism, while another school has set out to prove that Marx was not only omniscient but could predict the future. It is hard to tell which school has done more to render difficult a correct understanding of Marx's ideas.[6]

To try to prove Marx "omniscient" is a disservice to him, as it would be in the case of any scientist, but to deny his capacity for prediction is to deny his status as a scientist. Certainly many of the projections of Marx and Marxism have come to pass, not least the destruction of colonialism as part of the process of the undoing of capitalism—an essential theme of Davis' own book. And, happily, Davis leaves no doubt as to which of the two distortions has been at the same time most influential and most baneful.

Marxism may see certain social systems at certain epochs as having a progressive force, that is, as having the potential of enhancing productive capacity and, in a relative sense (relative to what it displaces), being able to insure significant social advances.

In that sense, a Marxist evaluation of such systems at such times will be positive, but this in no way denies Marxism's condemnation of the exploitative nature of such systems and of the inhuman features marking them. This applies, for example, both to systems of slavery in ancient times and to the advances of capitalist production relations throughout the world. But such evaluation should be confused neither with apologias for slaveholding (after all, when Marx's daughter asked him to name his heroes he mentioned two —Spartacus and Kepler!) nor for capitalism either as it functions in its original areas or, certainly, as it has functioned in its colonialist ventures.

A clear presentation of the multisided character of this development is in Marx's essay, "The Future Results of the British Rule in India," written on July 22, 1853.

The bourgeois period of history has to create the material basis of the new world—on the one hand the universal intercourse founded upon the mutual dependency of mankind, and the means of that intercourse; on the other hand the development of the productive powers of man and the transformation of material production into a scientific domination of natural agencies. Bourgeois industry and commerce create these material conditions of a new world in the same way as geological revolutions have created the surface of the earth. When a great social revolution shall have mastered the results of the bourgeois epoch, the market of the world and the modern powers of production, and subjected them to the common control of the most advanced peoples, then only will human progress cease to resemble that hideous pagan idol, who would not drink the nectar but from the skulls of the slain.[7]

This paragraph is preceded by a page in which Marx excoriated the British ruling class—"the men of 'Property, Order, Family, and Religion' "—exactly because in the ravishment of India all four had been trampled upon mercilessly. As he wrote: "The profound hypocrisy and inherent barbarism of bourgeois civilization lies unveiled before our eyes, turning from its home, where it assumes respectable forms, to the colonies, where it goes naked."[8]

Previous revolutions in the social order, then, have seen the displacement of one system by another and have registered human progress; but all of these systems have been—until socialism—

exploitative. They may have represented at their best periods progressive forces, but, since they remained exploitative and antagonistic and therefore basically antihuman, they were not themselves progressive systems.

For Marxism, everything begins and ends with man; its purpose is the ennoblement of human life. Its concept of man posits his historical evolvement, his social being; without man no society, without society no man. Its scientific sweep encompasses all phenomena: natural and social, collective and individual.

Speaking of the Marxist-Christian dialogue, Paul Oestreicher, a clergyman of the Church of England, affirms that "Its real significance must be in the context of a mutual recognition that both sides are committed to changing the world and fulfilling man. For that reason, the area in which certain consensus is essential is the understanding of the nature of man."[9] Similarly, Father Quentin Lauer, a Jesuit, and chairman of the Department of Philosophy at Fordham University, writes that "the 'credibility gap' between the two [Marxism and Christianity] will be narrowed only to the extent that each can convince the other that his own enterprise seriously and sincerely centers on man. If man is truly the point of convergence of the two enterprises, harmonious co-existence is not out of the question."[10]

On this crucial question of one's estimate of the species *homo sapiens* stands the Marxist estimate of man as like to a god, man having, indeed, made God. There is such a strand in religion, but the dominant note—as in Judaism and Christianity—is quite the contrary; in Job or in Paul and Augustine, Man is puerile, unknowing, with pride his greatest failing and—in Christianity more than in Judaism—the Fall induces innate and ineradicable proclivity toward sin, if not as in some views, the actuality of essential sinfulness.[11] It is exactly here—as to humankind and the interpretations of evil as well as in the estimate of knowledge (and in the especially demeaning approach to woman common to religion)—that some of the most fundamental distinctions between Marxism and religion appear.

Marxism's relationship to the humanist essence of the most advanced thinking of the eighteenth and nineteenth centuries is manifest in its entire corpus; a good expression of this appears in *The Holy Family,* written late in 1844 and first published the next year. A section from Marx reads:

> As *Cartesian* materialism merges into *natural science proper,* the other branch of French materialism leads directly to *socialism* and *communism.*
> There is no need of any great penetration to see from the teaching of materialism on the original goodness and equal intellectual endowment of men, the omnipotence of experience, habit and education, and the influence of environment on man, the great significance of industry, the justification of enjoyment, etc., how necessarily materialism is connected with communism and socialism. If man draws all his knowledge, sensation, etc., from the world of the senses and the experience gained in it, the empirical world must be arranged so that in it man experiences and gets used to what is really human and that he becomes aware of himself as man. . . . If man is shaped by his surroundings, his surroundings must be made human. If man is social by nature, he will develop his true nature only in society, and the power of his nature must be measured not by the power of separate individuals but by the power of society. (Marx's italics).[12]

Here, in this early writing, is also indicated Marxism's movement away from environmentalism and mechanical materialism, for emphasis already appears on the interaction between the environment and human beings, the impossibility of separating the social and the individual without damaging both, and the fact that the environment itself consists, in part, of man in society.

Among the attributes of the "really human" are not only reason and consciousness, not only labor and language—and labor that is planned and conscious. Not only the capacity to reason and plan, but also the capacity to resist and affirm is in the Marxist concept of "really human." Thus, for example, in *Capital,* when Marx is discussing slavery—and he has particularly in mind slavery in the United States—he writes:

> The laborer here is, to use a striking expression of the ancients, distinguishable only as an *instrumentum vocale,* from an animal as *instrumentum semivocale,* and from an implement as *instrumentum mutum.* But he himself takes care to let both beast and implement feel that he is none of them, but is a man. He convinces himself with immense satisfaction, that

he is a different being, by treating the one unmercifully and damaging the other *con amore.* [13]

Citing the work of J. E. Cairnes and Frederick L. Olmsted, Marx goes on to say that from this follows "the principle, universally applied in this method of production, [i.e., slavery] only to employ the rudest and heaviest implements and such as are difficult to damage owing to their sheer clumsiness."

This, incidentally, is an excellent illustration of the absurdity of identifying Marxism with economic determinism in the sense that Marx makes decisive in his choice of tools the subjective response of the user of those tools. [14]

The evidence suggests—contrary to the views of Bruno Bettelheim (and mechanically applying those views to slavery in the United States, as done, for example, by Stanley Elkins, which further compounds an error)—that resistance continued even in conditions prevailing in the Nazi concentration camps. Thus Primo Levi, writing of *Survival in Auschwitz,* recalls the words of a war prisoner during the First World War:

> ... that precisely because the *Lager* was a great machine to reduce us to beasts, we must not become beasts; that even in this place one can survive, and therefore one must want to survive, to tell the story, to bear witness; and that to survive we must force ourselves to save at least the skeleton, the scaffolding of civilization. We are slaves, deprived of every right, exposed to every insult, condemned to certain death, but we still possess one power, and we must defend it with all our strength for it is the last—the power to refuse our consent. [15]

Marx's concept of alienation, applied to labor, is founded upon the highest evaluation of man—wherefore he feels alienation. Where work is external to man, he is not himself when working and is therefore engaged in forced labor; "It is therefore not the satisfaction of a need; it is merely the *means* to satisfy needs external to it" (Marx's italics), Marx wrote. [16] In this sense the process was not only forced but was animal rather than human. Of course man must eat, and insofar as he has such needs he is an animal. Thus, "Certainly eating, drinking, procreating, etc., are also genuinely human functions. But in the abstraction which separates them from the

74

sphere of all other human activity and turns them into sole and ultimate ends, they are animal."

The point is: "Man makes his life-activity itself the object of his will and of his consciousness. He has conscious life-activity. It is not a determination with which he directly merges. Conscious life-activity directly distinguishes man from animal life-activity." The animal, on the other hand, "produces only under the dominion of immediate physical need," but "man produces even when he is free from physical need and only truly produces in freedom therefrom ... Man therefore also forms things in accordance with the laws of beauty."

In the same effort, Marx puts the fact of the individual and society—of man as social—in a classical form: "What is to be avoided above all is the re-establishing of 'Society' as an abstraction vis-a-vis the individual. The individual is *the social being.*"

It is pertinent to recall that Engels, writing at the same period and referring to the limitations of eighteenth-century materialism, observed that it "did not contend with the Christian contempt for and humiliation of Man, and merely posited Nature instead of the Christian God as the Absolute facing Man."[17] The point, however, for both Marx and Engels—and for Marxism—is that: "The criticism of religion ends, therefore, with the doctrine that *man is the supreme being for man,*" wherefore Marx announced his thunderous conclusion that facing Man was the need *"to overthrow all conditions* in which man is a degraded, enslaved, neglected, contemptible being ..." (Marx's italics).[18]

While Engels is correct in his description of "the Christian contempt," he is not, in that passage, presenting an all-encompassing view of the Christian approach. There is another, and an opposite, Christian position. Roger Garaudy has put these conflicting positions well:

The whole history of the Church is informed by this internal dialectic, by this opposition within it of the Constantinian tradition, in which the accent is on the fact of sin, and which serves as a justification for a providential and legitimate state or authority leading otherwise incapable men to liberty, and the apocalyptic tradition, which re-appears whenever the masses of the populace become aware of their strength, which places the

75

accent on the fact that God incarnate as Man has triumphed over sin, and which undertakes to inscribe this apocalypse into history.[19]

Essential to the chain-breaking potential in the great encyclical, *Pacem in Terris,* is that its entire emphasis is upon the anti-Constantine tradition. It begins, therefore, by affirming man's greatness, declaring that God "has created man intelligent and free," "establishing him as master of the universe." In keeping with this content, it quotes from Psalm 13, itself a prime witness to this strand in Christianity: "Thou has made him a little less than the angels: Thou has crowned him with glory and honor, and hast set him over the works of Thy hands. Thou has subjected all things under his feet."

Marxism's estimate of man is higher than this—Christianity goes no higher—for Marxism insists that man makes himself as well as God. Marxism does not ignore victimization; on the contrary, it springs out of the condemnation of such victimization and lives in order to end it. But Marxism affirms that while victimization is integral to all class-divided, exploitative societies, its result is not simply the victim but also the rebel. Victimization may induce fear and even apathy, but it may also provoke hatred for the oppressor and resistance to the oppression. Marxism declares not only that this *may* be the result, but that, historically, this has been and will continue to be the result. It will not be the only result, but the decisive result; the source of social dynamics lies in oppression only insofar as those oppressed respond actively to their condition. There is nothing automatic or mechanical about this; hence arises the extraordinary emphasis placed by Marxism upon consciousness and organization.

Certainly "Material force must be overthrown by material force. But theory also becomes a material force once it has gripped the masses. Theory is capable of gripping the masses when it demonstrates *ad hominem*, and it demonstrates *ad hominem* when it becomes radical. To be radical is to grasp things by the root. But for man the root is man himself."[20] It is this view that Nicholas Murray Butler labeled "crude, immoral and unhistorical"; it is this view, wrote Herbert Heaton, that denies that historical figures "were human beings" and turns them into "economic or social abstractions"; it is this view that cannot explain, according to Fred

M. Fling, why a man "should . . . sacrifice his life for an idea"; it is this view that, according to Jerome Frank, makes of humanity "merely ventriloquist dummies of inscrutable forces."[21]

How strangely these "ventriloquist dummies" have behaved, to whom human beings are mere abstractions! How idiotic of them, in the face of their own preconceived inscrutable forces, to resist the Bismarckian club, the Kuomintang terror, the FBI harrassments, and the fascist inquisition! What weird conduct all this is for these crude and amoral men and women, incapable of understanding why anyone—let alone they, themselves—should sacrifice life for an idea!

And how passionately have written the begetters of this robotlike, bloodless dogma: Engels on capitalism, "the despicable immorality of this system";[22] Marx,

With the development of capitalist production during the manufacturing period, the public opinion of Europe has lost the last remnant of shame and conscience. The nations bragged cynically of every infamy that served them as a means of capitalistic accumulation. . . . Liverpool waxed fat on the slave trade . . . the veiled slavery of the wage-workers in Europe needed, for its pedestal, slavery pure and simple in the new world. . . . If money, according to Augier, "comes into the world with a congenital blood-stain on one cheek," capital comes dripping from head to foot, from every pore, with blood and dirt.[23]

Statistics are not absent from the young Engels' account of *The Condition of the Working Class in England in 1844,* but its author's heat still lights those pages: "Close to the splendid houses of the rich such a lurking place of the bitterest poverty may be found"; "And how the poverty of these unfortunates, among whom even thieves find nothing to steal, is exploited by the property-holding class in lawful ways!"; ". . . the filth, the uninhabitableness of the houses and the neglect of the streets surpass all description." He already is denouncing the befouling of water and "the total pollution of the air"; to add to the almost weird modernity of the description, Engels writes of the center of the city with its teeming poor, the next zone with its "middle bourgeoisie," and further outside the core, the upper bourgeoisie in remoter villas with gardens . . . in free, wholesome country air, in fine comfortable homes . . . and the finest part of the arrangement is this, that the members of this money aristocracy can take the shortest road through the middle of all the laboring districts to their places of business, without ever seeing that they are in the midst of the grimy misery that lurks to the right and the left,[24]

for all the world like the limousines speeding over the thruway with Watts below or the expressway from Westchester County passing through Harlem to disgorge the bankers and brokers farther downtown!

In this same work, Engels denounces capitalism and its characteristic product, "the great towns" with their teeming and miserable masses. The inhabitants are "forced to sacrifice the best qualities of their human nature"; above all, wrote Engels, "a hundred powers which slumbered within them have remained inactive, have been suppressed. . . ." Engels also anticipates all the literature on the "loneliness of the crowd" and the depersonalization of metropolitan life when he writes of "the dissolution of mankind into monads. . . . Everywhere barbarous indifference, hard egotism on the one hand and nameless misery on the other . . . everywhere reciprocal plundering under the protection of the Law." And the sense of aimlessness, of purposelessness, of monotony—especially as they afflict the modern industrial worker—also recently "discovered" in a vast literature, is in this work of the 1840s, even in the same words, for Engels excoriates the "constraint," the "aimlessness," the "monotony" afflicting the worker; all these, he adds, "must make his work a torture . . . if he has the least human feeling left."[25]

The British scholar, John Lewis, is quite right when he insists that "There can be no place in the Marxist philosophy for any theory which rejects . . . the validity of those passionate feelings of moral indignation which were the driving force of Marx himself and of all his followers."[26] It is fitting that the single most beloved figure among contemporary Communists is Dolores Ibarruri of Spain, known to all as La Pasionaria.

Critics of Marxism, such as those cited earlier, hold not only to the view that it is amoral; they also insist that it posits an inevitable result reached without man's role or activity being consequential.

They feel that in this sense Marxism shows a kinship with the inevitability of some religious concepts, that is, results depending upon God's will and His alone and that man's actions are simply irrelevant in terms of the result.

This reflects a misunderstanding or a distortion of the Marxist view of inevitability that is, in fact, not fatalistic—independent of Man's acts—but is rather exactly the opposite of fatalism. That is, Marxist inevitability depends upon what men and women do. In the broadest sense, the demise of capitalism is felt to be certain because of its internal contradictions, but if one of the two contending parties—if the working class—does not successfully press forward, the conflict might, Marx and Engels warned, lead to mutual destruction, a warning that has a special poignancy to it in this age of thermonuclear weapons. Specifically, too, the Marxist emphasis upon what people do as an integral part of the concept of inevitability appears not only in party building and programmatic efforts, which constitute the entire political history of worldwide Marxist movement, but also in precise details. A typical example is the leaflet Marx wrote in September 1870 concerning the Franco-Prussian War, addressed to the members of the International Working Men's Association. He urged that all sections of the International, in defense of the Republic, "stir the working classes to action." And he warned—alas, with great accuracy—that: "If they forsake their duty, if they remain passive, the present tremendous war will be but the harbinger of still deadlier international feuds, and lead in every nation to a renewed triumph over the workman by the lords of the sword, of the soil, and of capital."[27]

Marxist confidence as to the inevitability of socialism, then, rests upon its confidence in how people will act, just as the physician's confidence in his prognosis depends upon how the patient acts. The sense of certainty therefore, far from being independent of humanity, of the result coming in spite of people, depends upon them and will come about only because of their practice.[28] This confidence derives, too, not only from convictions about how people will act but how they have acted; how, in fact, class struggle has recurred and has been decisive; how revolutions have occcurred and social systems have been displaced; how the oppressed have behaved in many different eras and areas; how—and most specifi-cally—capitalism and colonialism have been disintegrating and di-minishing and how socialism and national liberation have been appearing and spreading. This, however, is a confidence from within, as it were; it may reflect the readings of the past produced by an adherent of a particular view of that past and this present. These considerations, then, are particular; the former were general and theoretical and belong in an effort at dialogue with those whose views differ and particularly with those who, being religious, tend to reject a view that begins and ends with man and nothing else.

It should be added that this confidence does not rest on any assumption that man is nothing but a rational phenomenon, the idea that irrational behavior is not for him. On the contrary irra-tional behavior—that is, behavior contrary to reality and/or inter-est—is common, and would be particularly common where one has exploitative societies whose maintenance depends in part upon the promulgation of ideas that are obscurantist, antiscientific, elitist, cynical and/or misanthropic. The point is not to deny that irration-ality exists; the point is to distinguish between the irrational and the inexplicable. It is the latter that Marxism denies.

Affirming that phenomena are—by their nature, if not (yet) by the extent of human knowledge—subject to explication confirms the materialist base of this outlook and the insistence that philoso-phy's task is not simply to comprehend (though this, too, means to explicate) but to change the world, and that means that not only diagnosis but also prognosis are possible. Perhaps an illustration is in order. Racism is irrational insofar as its substance is antiscien-tific, is untrue. Racism also is irrational in the sense that when it appears among whites who are themselves among the exploited it serves (and is meant to serve) a divisive function, making such exploitation easier to maintain and intensify. This does not mean, however, that the appearance of racism in the first place cannot be explicated in sociohistoric terms; and it does not mean, secondly, that its hold upon whites whose class and social position ought to make them resist it cannot also be explained in terms of history, social pressures, legal requirements, psychological and physical forms of intimidation, educational and propagandistic (including "religious") indoctrination, and so on. Such an approach is vital to a comprehension of the phenomenon and is indispensable if one is to attempt in any organized way to eliminate the offending irrationality.

As Marxism rejects an exclusive environmentalism, so it also rejects an exclusive subjectivism, whether in the form of Freudianism or in related concepts of innate aggressiveness, as projected recently by Desmond Morris, Robert Ardrey and Konrad Lorenz.[29] This rejection is based on the dialectical principles of interaction and interpenetration, on a reading of history that emphasizes a capacity for development and progress while recognizing the realities of obstacles and oppression, on what are held to be the most persuasive findings in such areas as anthropology, biology, and zoology, and on class viewpoint that not only sees the objective relationship between the liberation of the most oppressed and the emancipation of humanity, but that also affirms the purifying and strengthening qualities present in enduring privation and resisting oppression.

The insistence upon innate depravity—as by the writers just named—continues one of the elements present in religion, notably in powerful elements of Christian thought. For example, in Romans 7:18–24 one reads:

> For I know that in me (that is, in my flesh,) dwelleth no good thing: for to will is present with me; but how to perform that which is good I find not.
> For the good that I would do I do not: but the evil that I would not, that I do.
> Now if I do that I would not, it is no more I that do it, but sin that dwelleth in me.
> I find then a law, that, when I would do good, evil is present with me.
> For I delight in the law of God after the inward man:
> But I see another law in my members, warring against the law of my mind, and bringing me into captivity to the law of sin which is in my members.
> O wretched man that I am! who shall deliver me from the body of this death?

This also reflects the sharp duality in much of religious thought as well as its tendency to make of sin that which is "fleshly," thus identifying with sexuality; more will be said of this later. However, while noting this strand here, attention again is called to the contrary view in religion, a view indicated in the quotations Pope John XXIII chose for *Pacem in Terris*. It is in the books of the Bible that one reads that the last shall become the first and the first last; that the meek shall inherit the earth; that the rich will have great difficulty entering heaven; that God so loved the enslaved that he parted the seas to help them escape, and that he so hated slaveowners he closed the seas upon them and drowned them.

This is in Marx and in Lenin. They hold to the liberating essence of the exploited and the oppressed basically because of their position in society and the lever that that position affords them with which to bring about transformation. They are at the center of contradiction, and only changing their status makes possible the ending of that contradiction. Also present, however, is the idea that since they are not among the exploiters and the oppressors they are of a superior mold compared to those who are so situated. They have not undergone corruption; they have experienced a common suffering and developed a sense of solidarity and a feeling of competence that makes of them better human beings—more human.

This concept is present among exploited peoples themselves; it forms, for example, a fundamental thread in both the creative and the historical literature of the Afro-American people, and it is part of the marrow within such peoples as the Irish (compared to the English) and of the Jews (compared to those who oppress them).[30] This idea—and the idea in Marxism-Leninism—does not deny the dehumanizing potential in impoverishment and extreme persecution, but it does deny that this is all there is or that this is triumphant, and it insists on the dialectical quality of such suffering insofar as it has brought about and does bring about resistance thereto.

Here, too, an example will be useful. In Virginia in 1800, many slaves were involved in a conspiracy to rebel. Leaders were apprehended, with more or less difficulty, and many were sentenced to various forms of punishment, including execution. Contemporary evidence demonstrated that the rebels desired "death or liberty"; that, as one of them said, "We have as much right to fight for our liberty as any men"; that, wrote a contemporary, "Of those who have been executed, no one has betrayed his cause. They have uniformly met death with fortitude." The character of the rebels and their goal caused conscience-searching on the part of the one-time rebel who was then Governor of Virginia. He wrote to another who had played a leading role in a bloody revolution, had written an immortal manifesto of rebellion, and who was soon to be elected President of the United States; James Monroe wrote to Thomas Jefferson, asking his advice about the pending execution of many of the black rebels. Jefferson replied, urging mercy, suggesting that the Governor not "go one step beyond necessity." He urged this course since "the world at large . . . cannot lose sight of the rights of the two parties, & the object of the unsuccessful one."[31]

Is it possible that those who persistently have right on their side and battle for it and that those who do not and battle against it do not, thereby, affect their respective characters and psychologies?

In a recent editorial (May 26, 1969), The *Nation* commented upon the forced resignation of Justice Abe Fortas: "When we make *things* and their *possession* the measure of success, we become enthralled with things, and in our captivity continue to grasp for more things, more power. . . . We have become a nation of salesmen, brokers and expediters; we lack one single Jeremiah to save our souls." The condemnation is merited, but its all-enveloping nature, while typical of liberal lamentation, is not in accordance with reality. In this very editorial, indeed, the *Nation* observed that "many young people" are in rebellion against this barbarism; one may add many among the working people, as the coal miners of West Virginia, the Indians of the Northwest, the chicanos of the Southwest, and the twenty-five million black people in the United States. They are not "salesmen, brokers and expediters;" their blood has not been turned the color of money; and they constitute millions upon millions of Jeremiahs whose positions make necessary and natural their battle to save the soul of our Republic.

It is not often that one finds confirmation of an anti-elitist view —basic to both early Christianity and Marxism—from important

83

American business executives; indeed, as one would expect, one normally gets the opposite. This makes all the more remarkable the extraordinary condemnation of elitism that issued some years back from John Rhodes, vice-president of Interstate Wells, writing in, of all places, the *Harvard Business Review.* "What I find," said this rather unique corporation executive,

is an industrial economy which should be the despair of any deep thinker. Its broad base is populated by all kinds of people, uneducated and educated, but essentially good and kind. But as soon as you rise above the lowest levels, you begin to see why Jesus taught resignation and humility rather than ambition. Ambition turns these ordinary, kindly people into something almost unnatural. For from the first supervisory levels to the top, industry is shot through with monsters who do not know they are evil, who through indifference, neglect, or deliberate intention perpetrate cruelties that are the more horrible because undramatic . . . a denial of participation, a lack of natural love and affection, a thwarting of brotherhood, a suppression of creativity . . . suspicion, greed, envy . . . no sense of identification, of belonging. . . . There may be kindliness above, but right down the line there is indifference, jealousy, and downright cruelty . . . a staggering total of evil. . . ."[32]

That one finds a veritable Jeremiah whose warnings are printed in the *Harvard Business Review* bespeaks the horrors inducing them and the still viable impact of the revolutionary traditions that fill both Testaments of the Bible; these are fundamental to the humanistic concerns that permeate the teachings of Moses, Jesus, Buddha —and Marx.[33]

Chapter Six

Reason and Religion

Marxism is wedded to science, and science is the quintessence of reason. Religion, on the other hand, traditionally and dominantly, is suprarational and, indeed, antireason and antiscience. The latter strain is mixed with one that insists not only upon man's incapacity but also his inherent defectiveness, his sinfulness. Here, too, Marxism stands in sharp contrast; its position on man's capacity and effectiveness is the opposite of that which has traditionally characterized the religious stance. From these two strands in religion logically flows a third: acquiescence to the status quo, with efforts to alter it—on whatever grounds—being denounced because they would be ineffective, they would reflect upon God's work, they would manifest the sin of vanity and the terrible failing of pride, and because they would display a lack of faith. I have said that other and, indeed, contrary concepts appear in religion, but the above have been dominant and certainly have been controlling in most religious institutions for most of their history.

In Genesis the devil's agent, the snake, seduces woman (typically, for religious writings, she yields first), and she persuades man to eat the fruit of the Tree of Knowledge; this produces the loss of innocence and the Fall, and it is from this disaster—this defiance of God—that sinfulness stems, that all are cursed, and that death becomes humanity's common fate.[1]

The point in the Book of Job is that despite reason, despite experience, despite "common sense," despite all arguments concerning evil as retribution or as testing or as preparation, and despite the urgings of his wife (again!), Job finally believes exactly because God, in a personal encounter, shows him how little he knows and how little he can know and that Job's urge to understand is itself a colossal failing. The point is that you cannot understand, and exactly because you cannot, therefore you must believe; in doing so, Job vindicates God and again he bests Satan.

In his early work, *The Book of Job as a Greek Tragedy* (1918), Horace Kallen drew from his reading the lesson that man's essence was integrity; but this is a forced reading, I think, unless one defines integrity in the manner Job did (Job 27:5f.), integrity as "my righteousness," that is, his faith in God, no matter what. Hayim Greenberg was at the mark when he wrote: "The true believer practices the most heroic defiance in the world. His logic may be strange and paradoxical, as in the case of Job, who declared, 'Even though He slay me will I believe in Him.' Those who regard such an attitude as absurd cannot be proved wrong, but people who reason thus have nothing to do with religion"[2]—at least, nothing to do with religion as defined by Greenberg. One should add that while Job was ready to give his life God did not require this; He took, rather, only the lives of his servants and his children, and what they may have thought of the bargain is not recorded in Job.

One remembers that God tested Abraham by ordering him to "take thy son, thy only son, Isaac, whom thou lovest, and slay him," and that thereupon Abraham laid his son upon an altar and put a knife to his throat; but because he was obedient, quite beyond the dimensions of human reason, the Lord stopped the sacrifice.

The message of Ecclesiates is accurately delineated by Arthur C. Cochrane when he sees in it "not reason but revelation."[3] The preacher finally understood that in applying "my mind to know" he was pursuing the course of "madness and folly," for all this was "but a striving after wind." Explicitly: "For in much wisdom is much vexation, and he who increases knowledge increases sorrow" (Ecclesiastes 1:16–18).

To the question that, being unable to resist God's will, how can God find fault with us, the reply of Paul is the reply of Job: "Who are you, a man, to answer back to God: . . . Has the potter no right over the clay, to make out of the same lump one vessel for beauty and another for menial use?" (Romans 9:20–21).

Luther, in his last sermon (1546), called reason "the devil's bride" and "an accursed whore," again making it feminine in terms of its terrible seductiveness. This is deep not only in religion in general but in religion as preached in the United States. In one of the earliest sermons on the then-colonial soil, Thomas Hooker, talking to "The Activity of Faith" (1651), argued: "We must blind the eye of carnal reason, resolve to obey, though heaven and earth seem to meet together in a contradiction."[4] This urging was brought forward specifically to suggest the propriety of resignation in the face of suffering and oppression; "the more misery, the greater mercy"; those who suffer much but bear all without complaint and without question "shall receive a double reward . . . even a crown of glory." (Job, it may be recalled, is promised nothing at all, which is a difference between the so-called Old and New Testaments; on the other hand, when Job passes all the tests, God does reward him on earth—with more children and abundance of cattle!)[5]

The same theme is central to the philosophy of Thomas Aquinas, declared by Leo XIII in his encyclical *Aeterni Patris* (1879) to be the official philosophy of the Roman Catholic church. Thus, arguing that "sacred doctrine" is "nobler" than what he calls "other sciences," Aquinas urges that this is because "sacred doctrine" surpasses the others

. . . in point of greater certitude, because other sciences derive their certitude from the natural light of human reason, which can err, while this derives its certitude from the light of the divine knowledge, which cannot be deceived; in point of the higher worth of its subject-matter, because this science treats chiefly of those things which by their sublimity transcend human reason, while other sciences consider only those things which are within reason's grasp.

(Aquinas adds that its purpose—eternal happinesss—also makes it more noble.)

At several other points this theme is repeated and intensified; thus: "Matters of faith are above human reason and so we cannot attain to them except through grace"; "Since man's nature is dependent on a higher nature, natural knowledge does not suffice for its perfection and some supernatural knowledge is necessary. . . ."; "In many respects faith perceives the invisible things of God in a higher way than natural reason. . . ."; "It is necessary for man to accept by faith not only things which are above reason, but also those things which can be known by reason . . . ," etc.[6]

Calvin made of man all stench and filth; should he here or hereafter receive anything other than pain it flows only from the ultimate and inexplicable goodness of God. Hence, again, resignation, obedience, and faith were the only significant virtues, and their absence—especially belief in man's capacities—the serious vices.

Again, dominant religious teaching in the United States follows these leads. Nathaniel W. Taylor (1786–1858), for many years a professor at Yale, in a sermon at the Yale chapel in 1828 excoriated "the wicked heart—the sinful disposition of men." The source of all abominations, he taught, lay in "man's free, voluntary preference of the world as his chief good." It was the source insofar as it was at the heart of man's ineradicable depravity and it resulted in abominations insofar as it led to vain and sinful efforts at societal improvements. The latter point was spelled out in detail:

So of mankind, change their circumstances as you may; place them where you will within the limits of their being; do what you will to prevent the consequence, you have one uniform result, entire moral depravity. No change of condition, no increase of light nor of motives, no instructions, nor warnings, no any thing, within the appropriate circumstances of their being, changes the result. Unless there be some interposition, which is not included in these circumstances, unless something be done which is above nature, the case is hopeless. Place a human being any where within the appropriate limits and scenes of his immortal existence, and such is his nature, that he will be a depraved sinner.[7]

Charles P. Krauth (1823–1883), one of the most influential Lutheran teachers in American history, in his magnum opus *The Conservative Reformation and Its Theology,* insisted on the exclusion of reason as the heart of religion and the consequent need for faith as the saving element. Thus he says: "The atonement, in its whole conception, belongs to a world which man cannot now enter. The blessings and adaptations of it we can comprehend in some measure. We can approach them with tender hearts full of gratitude; but the *essence* of the atonement we can understand as little as we can understand the essence of God."[8]

Perhaps as prolific as Krauth and even more influential was Charles Hodge (1797–1878), an almost permanent fixture at the Princeton Presbyterian Seminary; his great work, in three volumes, is *Systematic Theology* (1871–72).[9] The fundamentalist approach that continues as dominant in the United States, certainly in the various hierarchies and probably among most members of congregations, is at the heart of *Systematic Theology.* Two paragraphs from the first volume read:

It is plain that complete havoc must be made of the whole system of revealed truth, unless we consent to derive our philosophy from the Bible, instead of explaining the Bible by our philosophy. If the Scriptures teach that sin is hereditary, we must adopt a theory of sin suited to that fact. If they teach that men cannot repent, believe, or do anything spiritually good, without the supernatural aid of the Holy Ghost, we must make our theory of moral obligation accord with that fact.

Protestants hold, (1) That the Scriptures of the Old and New Testaments are the Word of God, written under the inspiration of the Holy Ghost, and are therefore infallible, and of divine authority in all things pertaining to faith and practice, and consequently free from all error whether of doctrine, fact or precept. (2) That they contain all the extant supernatural revelations of God designed to be a rule of faith and practice to his Church. (3) That they are sufficiently perspicuous to be understood by the people, in the use of ordinary means and by the aid of the Holy Spirit, in all things necessary to faith or practice, without the need of any infallible interpreter.

Within religion in general, as has been stressed, there are contrary themes, and within religion as preached and practiced in the United States these contrary themes, while never dominant, have been very significant and even potent. In the mainstream of white, Christian, rather affluent America such variations have appeared. Especially notable as a force of this character was William Ellery Channing (1780–1842), the symbol of Unitarian Christianity. As minister at the Federal Street Church in Boston and as a nationally known lecturer and author his ideas decisively influenced such people as Emerson, Longfellow, William Cullen Bryant, Charles Sumner, Lydia Maria Child, Horace Mann, and Dorothea Dix.

It is not so much differences concerning the Trinity that basically set apart Channing—and those influenced by him who further developed his ideas; it is rather Channing's rejection of the God-centered religion of orthodoxy for a religion centered on humanity. From this followed a concern with secular arrangements, a repugnance toward all forms of mystification and superstition, and a flexibility that appealed strongly to the rational rather than the supernatural. *The Perfect Life*, published first in 1873 through the efforts of his nephew, presents his two basic themes:

> Lay it down then as a primary, fundamental truth, that to a moral being there is but one essential enduring Good—and that is, the health, power and purity of his own soul. Hold this doctrine intelligently, and you hold the key that is gradually to unlock to you the mysteries of nature and providence, of duty, temptation and happiness, of this life and the life to come.

> Christianity should now be disencumbered and set free from the unintelligible and irrational doctrines, and the uncouth and idolatrous forms and ceremonies, which terror, superstition, vanity, priestcraft and ambition have labored to identify with it. It should come forth from the darkness and corruption of the past in its own celestial splendor, and in its divine simplicity. It should be comprehended *as having but one purpose, the perfection of human nature, the elevation of men into nobler beings.* (Italics added.)

From there a rather straight line leads to Walter Rauschenbusch, Harry F. Ward, Christian socialism (in the United States), Norman Thomas (trained first as a minister), A. J. Muste, and Claude Williams.[10]

The traditional and dominant Roman Catholic approach to questions of reason, sin, and social change can also be illustrated in terms of the United States in particular. No more characteristic and significant example suggests itself than that of George Dering Wolff, founder and, for many years, editor of the *American Catholic Quarterly Review*. In July 1878, he wrote on "Socialistic Communism in the United States," moved to this by the tremendous stirrings of the 1870s and not least by the great strikes of 1877. Wolff made clear that his objection to socialism was based upon its rejection of what he held to be the fundamental Catholic idea, namely, that the evil in the world arose out of the corruption in men's hearts, that salvation through faith and through consenting "to the truth" offered by the church was the only way such evil could be countered. This capacity for salvation for all, through faith and the church, contrasted with "one of the dominating errors of Protestantism," that is, its insistence upon "the total depravity and corruption of human nature, and the cold, stern rigid Calvinism which is the logical result of this error."

But in the United States and elsewhere, Wolff continued, Protestantism had "swung over to the opposite extreme," for now it was "denying the positive existence of sin as an inherent element in fallen humanity, and the need of divine grace to regenerate it." Especially in New England was this error committed, and this was the more tragic as New England "was the center of intellectual light to the whole of the United States." Hence "humanitarianism became the prevalent religion." Thus: "The development of humanity by its own powers and capacities was the grand idea. The causes of evil were all external to our nature. 'Excelsior' was the cry. With more perfect social arrangements man would improve, advance, develop, mount upwards, and soar into the empyrean. ..."

Schools created after this New England heresy—"in which man himself was set forth as the supreme object of worship, the ideal of human life"—have become transmitters of socialism therefore, and their textbooks are seditious as well as heretical. The schools and that religion teach discontent with the present condition of man and society and teach egalitarianism; these are ideas from the devil. Remedies for human and societal ills "cannot possibly consist in any alterations or changes in the industrial, social, or political relations of men. ... The cause of the trouble is not external to human

91

nature; consequently an external remedy will be powerless."

On this basis, the function of religion—truly understood—as reconciler of the poor and the oppressed to their earthly suffering is spelled out in explicit terms that read as almost a satire on "opiate" concepts of religion. Thus we are told:

> Christianity in the Church takes hold of the poor. To them the Gospel is especially preached. It limits and regulates their desire for temporal comfort. It teaches them resignation, submission to Providence, not as a vague powerless sentiment, but as a positive duty . . . thus the fire of wicked passions which toil, suffering, and privation engender is quenched, useless longing and ambitious desires for a condition beyond reach are repressed, and vain strugglings after what cannot be obtained are suppressed . . . acquiescence in what is recognized as providential circumstances drives out discontent, jealousy, hatred, and the other wicked passions to which discontent and inordinate ambition give rise.[11]

The radical strain in early Christianity and in Catholicism has also been marked in the United States from the early Orestes Browning and T. Wharton Collens to today's Berrigan brothers and Dorothy Day. As before, the essential point of difference was the central concern with humanity on earth, with the God who came in the flesh, with His work being to make Jerusalem here. Precious little difference marks a Harvey Cox from a James Colaianni or a Richard Shaull from a Michael Novak or a Eugene Bianchi from a Joseph Fletcher or a Peter Riga from a Robert Goldburg.

Insofar as religion speaks in the manner of Nathaniel Taylor or George Wolff, Marxism repudiates it and attacks it as vigorously as their views reject Marxism. Insofar as religion per se contains within itself a rejection of reason or a projection of that which is "superior" to reason, in terms of comprehension Marxism rejects it. Insofar, however, as religion strives for but "one purpose, the perfection of human nature, the elevation of men [and women] into nobler beings," Marxism would affirm a substantially similar ultimate purpose.

The distinguished Czech theologian and philosopher, Jan M. Lochman, sees several points of "convergence" between Christianity and Marxism; I agree with his points although I think the term "convergence" is excessive. Points of similarity surely exist: both

92

hold "man is a social creature," "both take history seriously," both have "thinking directed to the future." But precisely on the question of God and His existence Lochman sees the basic divergence, and again I think he is substantially correct. And it is raised here because it goes directly to the point of reason and man's primacy.

Lochman says he does not raise this question of God in terms of divergence with reference "to a metaphysical concept of God"; no, he says that the God he has in mind "is not the God of a metaphysical scheme, but the God of history, of society, of the future"—but all defined specifically in terms of the Gospel of Christ. It is not clear from this what Lochman proposes to do with the portion of mankind who are religious and who do not accept as their religion that of Christ's Gospel; or what he plans to do with those who are not religious at all, whether it be Christ's Gospel or the messages of Moses or others. What he has in mind he places in italics, *"the transcendence of grace."* And he holds that this transcendence "does not alienate man" but that rather it *"does* free him for history, for social life, for the future." The italics make clear what Lochman finds important but they do not help in explicating these ideas; they do not make them reasonable; they do not divest these ideas of faith and of the kind of assertion that refuses proof or demonstration.

Lochman writes that Marxism's disavowal of the question of God had as one source its awareness that the question had been employed as a means for "the improper turning away from man's concrete and worldly obligations." He adds that because the history of religion shows so often its "misuse," Marxism "has solid grounds for its atheism." For, he agrees, "Dedication to the great task of the revolutionary refashioning of this world must not be watered down with 'pious reasons.'" But this is not the main source of Marxism's disavowal of the question of God. The disavowal is based upon the insistence that man creates God and does so as the necessary expression of his humanity in a world that is exploitative and oppressive and in the midst of a natural environment that often seems harsh and always inexplicable. In this sense, God is an expression of man's incapacity and alienation at the same that His creation is a form of protest against both. Therefore, the institutionalizing of religion in class societies makes its usual use, historically, that which Lochman admits, namely, a main bastion supporting a foul status quo.

But Lochman is saying something else, too, and Marxists must listen with great care, for the errors and crimes committed in the name of Marxism have already been numerous and awful. In this connection it is surely not coincidental that Lochman writes also as a Czech, for failings there have been emphasized on all sides and denied by none, however explanations and remedies may differ. Lochman argues his own case thus:

> If God is ideologically denied, then man is threatened to become dissolved in his history, society and his future and he becomes imprisoned in his immanence and his worldly projects. The penultimate becomes the ultimate for him. His total destiny then depends on his accomplishments. . . . Over against all this the Christian message speaks of the transcendence of grace as the ultimate dimension of human existence. The *transcendence:* man is never used up completely in his social and historical conditions. His future is greater than the future of his accomplishments.

"The ultimate," writes Lochman, "the proper future of man, is grace." He holds:

> the real task of Christians in their encounter with Marxists appears to me to testify to this condition of being human. . . . If the church fashions and promulgates "laws" instead of this message, then she understands herself as an ideological antipower set against Marxism (and how often has she done so!). If she does that, then she misses her unique and most distinctive contribution and witness for the society: she becomes worthless salt.[12]

Marxism acknowledges nothing over man and Lochman does nothing to make clear, to explicate, to present rationally his key terms, *transcendence* and *grace,* let alone the particular Christian definitions that he has in mind for both. Marxism does not hold that "man is used up completely in his social and historical conditions." Those conditions—and they include all states, including the psychological, the emotional, and so on—are not "used up"; they are projected and form part of a seamless and endless web of time and history. To the web each contributes or detracts, and there is no sense of being "used up." There is a moment of termination for each, but there is no termination for the process, and each is or has been or will be part of that process. How he understands it, and how he acts on it and in it depends decisively—not wholly, but decisively—upon himself. Here there is no room for or need of an inexplicable "grace" coming from no one knows where and doing no one knows what, that is, by definition, being beyond understanding.

Where Marxists have acted mechanically and vulgarly—and some have at some periods and some places—the fault is in them, and to the degree that it exists they are acting contrary to Marxism. The sharpness of the struggle and the temptations presented by that struggle, let alone the temptations offered by possessing power, may induce such abominable behavior. To the degree that this is so, the function of a religious person or the function of religion as indicated by Lochman is salutary. It will help remind all, including Marxists, of the purpose of Marxism: the ennoblement of life; and it will help the Marxists remember how complex is life and how infinitely evolving is the process and the very definition of ennoblement.

In the collective is realized the individual; in selflessness is completed the self; in service is compensation; in work well loved and well done is life; in struggling against every indignity and oppression is fulfillment. For the Marxist, this is his "ultimate."

Chapter Seven

Sex, Women, and Religion

Joseph Wood Krutch, writing almost fifty years ago, declared that "the early Christian Fathers were wrong in assuming that the human race would have been better off if it had been able to propagate itself by means of some harmless system of vegetation."[1] Augustine, who saw the essence of human degradation manifested in sexual appetite, and decided that the basis for both perpetual punishment and perpetual guilt lay in sexual intercourse, was only somewhat more extreme in his hostility toward sex and more imaginative in his denunciations of its manfestations than others among the Fathers. But in Christianity—and in Judaism, though there to a lesser degree—sex was the great evil temptation and yielding to it practically synonymous with sin per se.

The tradition of the separation of soul from body, of the spiritual from the material, with the first the purer and the immortal—all going well—and the latter the corrupt and fated for disintegration, emerged as the condemnation of flesh, of the carnal.[2] Hence the virginal, the pure, and the immaculate applied to the absence of sexual intercourse and the presence of not only virtue but cleanliness; in the latter sense, there is more than one meaning to the phrase, "cleanliness is next to Godliness." Except for such concepts as original sin, the inferiority of women, and racism, it is likely that this equating of sex with sin has caused more human travail than any other notion.[3]

A generation and a half ago, Bertrand Russell reported that a friend of his had "made a statistical investigation into the ethical valuations of undergraduates in certain American colleges." "Most considered," Russell continued, "Sabbath-breaking more wicked than lying, and extra-conjugal sexual relations more wicked than murder."[4] It is likely that the past forty or fifty years have seen greater changes here, as elsewhere, than was true in the thousand or twelve hundred years preceding the above survey. Thus, the penitential books in use in the seventh and eighth centuries provided the following ecclesiastical punishments: for gluttony and drunkenness, a penitential fast of from three to forty days; for homicide, from one month to ten years depending upon motives and circumstances; for sexual "sins," from three to forty years, or even for life, depending upon their gravity, repetitiousness, and so on.[5]

Views on sex and sexual behavior attributed to Marxism vary wildly. Some affirm them to be rather puritanical or Victorian; others feel that Marxism's debasement is shown most clearly in its attitude of "abandon" toward sex, with stories of the communalization of women being but one illustration of the more vivid imaginings by—probably—repressed folk.

The lives of Marx, Engels, and Lenin certainly reflect nothing of either abandonment or of puritanism. While practices in socialist societies soon after revolution sometimes have shown extremes—in both directions, often—the dominant Marxist attitude toward sex is that it is delightful and that, at its best, its most moving and satisfying, it reflects the expression of mature devotion between a man and a woman. Any trace of "surrender" or "conquest," any trace of duress or force (physical, psychological, socioeconomic, and the like) is wrong, and any manifestation of male supremacy in the act is vile.

One may observe here that the "means of production" are irrevocably in private possession. Hence, while social considerations are manifestly present, particularly in terms of the special needs of women—such as birth control, abortion, and so on—and of chil-

98

dren, the individual and the private dominate; therefore, a good working rule would appear to be that the exercise of sexuality is the privilege and pleasure of adults and is the business of two such adults and nobody else's. On the whole this would answer the question of so-called "perversions," though the attitude toward homosexuality remains rather intensely hostile in socialist countries.

Such sexual conduct as well as the extraordinary emphasis upon sexuality in the West, and especially in the United States, (particularly in rather exotic and sadistic forms) is viewed by Marxists as a reflection of decadence. Manifestations of this in civilizations in decline—as in the Greek and Roman empires, or in those of Nazi Germany and fascist Italy—serve to confirm this analysis, especially as far as dominant American cultural and behavioral patterns are concerned.

Pornography is viewed as that form of literature or cinema or drama in which sexuality is demeaned—and made rather boring—because it is the activity of nonhuman beings, that is, males and females with no problems, no feelings (in general or for each other), and no functions (except genital). A work is pornographic only if it is debasing or bestial in almost a literal sense. Pornography is also normally characterized by the grossest manifestations of male supremacy and in this way, too, is offensive. The obvious commercial motivations in the pornographic production is an additional feature that makes it nauseating in the Marxist view.

Class societies being male supremacist, women were held to be inferior to men in nature, and therefore properly so in fact and in law. Religion, mirroring and generally bulwarking the status quo, agrees with the idea of woman's inferiority; its attitude toward sexuality intensified this idea. There is something paradoxical here, for the same literature that excoriated woman in terms of her identification with sexuality and its identification with sinfulness simultaneously emphasized that men were more sexual, more easily aroused and more preoccupied with sexuality, than women. This very allegation was in turn used to maintain male dominance and to help blight the lives of women. This paradox was resolved in theory, however, by insisting that it was woman who was the temptress, and in that sense her very nature, her very appearance, was the source of sin. Classically, of course, this is reflected in the Garden of Eden and the woman there as the cause of the Fall; again the logic is faulty, since in that story woman succumbed to the devil, while man succumbed to mere woman. The illogic is normally overcome, however, by insisting that this shows woman to be the agent of the devil while man is only the victim of that agent.

Since class and male supremacist societies long antedate Christianity, attitudes and even details of the antiwoman approach appear long before Christ. An example is the insistence of Sirach (200–175 B.C.) that "From a woman was the beginning of sin; and because of her we all die." A feature of the regularly repeated prayer by the Orthodox Jewish male was to thank God for having made the prayerful one a man and a not a woman. In the Old Testament, the wife is included among the man's possessions and is always a minor legally; no woman can inherit except in the absence of male heirs, and any oath by a female required the consent of a male adult to be considered valid.

In Christianity, the assumption of the Lord's maleness is plain and His incarnation is his Son; similarly all angels are given male names and with almost no exceptions all officials of all churches are male. Indeed, among certain of the Fathers—such as Jerome and Ambrose—to the degree that woman became truly religious she became male; if she truly serves Christ, said Jerome, she "will cease to be a woman and will be called man (*vir*)." Ambrose, in the same vein, suggested that "she who believes progresses to perfect manhood, to the measure of the adulthood of Christ . . . [and] dispenses with the name of her sex. . . ."[6] Paul held that "man is not made from woman, but woman from man. Neither was man created for woman, but woman for man." And in I Timothy 2:9–15, if it is not Paul himself who speaks, the sentiments certainly are Pauline; "Let a woman learn in silence with all submissiveness. I permit no woman to teach or to have authority over men; she is to keep silent. . . . Yet woman will be saved through bearing children, if she also be subject in everything to their husbands."

The Fathers held women to be inferior—garrulous, weak-minded, unstable; some, indeed, believed that women were not really human.[7] In any case, "Wives, be subject to your husbands, as to the Lord" (Ephesians 5:22–24); Augustine, Aquinas, and Jerome agreed; the latter taught: "For love befits the man; fear befits the woman." He added: "As for the slave, not only fear is befitting him, but also trembling," but this is a matter to be examined at some length further on.

Literal insistence upon woman as Satan's emissary is not wanting in the "sacred" literature. Tertullian said of woman, "You are the devil's gateway. . . . How easily you destroyed man, the image of God. Because of the death you brought upon us, even the Son of God had to die." In the sixteenth century, Ignatius of Loyola, the founder of the Jesuit Order, announced a marked resemblance between Satan—the enemy—and woman; indeed, he found: "The enemy conducts himself as a woman. He is a weakling before a show of strength, and a tyrant if he has his will."

Traditionally the modern Catholic church—excluding the exceptional John XXIII—has confirmed male supremacist evaluation of woman. Leo XIII attacked socialism because, among many other "crimes," it questioned "paternal authority" (1878), and he refuted this with an appropriate quotation from Paul. In *Rerum Novarum* (1891), the Pope announced again the Church's finding that woman "is by nature fitted for home work"; between these two statements, he had explicitly stated that the wife "must be subject to her husband and obey him" (1880).

In fascist Italy—with the extreme male supremacist attitude that characterizes fascism—Pius XI denounced coeducation as being "founded upon naturalism and the denial of original sin" (1929). He saw in it "a deplorable confusion of ideas that mistakes a leveling promiscuity and equality for the legitimate association of the sexes." The Pope went on to insist that there must not be "promiscuity, and much less equality, in the training of the two sexes." Mary Daly acutely notes that here the Pope seems to be deploring equality even more than promiscuity! A year late in another encyclical, this same Pope, speaking of a virtuous domestic order (writing from Rome in the midst of fascist Italy), declared: "This order

101

includes both the primacy of the husband with regard to the wife and children, [and] the ready subjection of the wife and her willing obedience."

The present Pope, Paul VI, has reaffirmed traditional Church positions in his attitudes toward birth control, divorce, and abortion; his remarks on woman show that such attitudes rest upon the traditional male supremacist estimate of woman as such. She is, he said in October 1966, while addressing the delegates to a meeting of Italian physicians, "the creature most docile," and must be protected from such vile practices as divorce—itself, the Pope said, "a sign of pernicious moral decadence."[8]

While Pius XI was reaffirming in Mussolini's Italy the traditional three k's for women, it became a central theme of nazism. A best seller in Hitler's Germany (first published there in 1934 and selling 100,000 copies in short order) was Gertrude von le Fort's *The Eternal Woman*, which has since been translated into French, Italian, Spanish, Portuguese, and English, and sells very widely, with full Church approval, where those languages are used. The English edition was issued by Bruce in Milwaukee as recently as 1962; the theme of the book is the necessity and propriety of woman's complete subjection.

Monsignor George A. Kelly, writing as director of the Family Life Bureau in the Archdiocese of New York and with the assurance of expertise that only a life vowed to celibacy makes possible, takes a position in his *Catholic Marriage Manual* that is only slightly less insulting toward men than women:

"Nothing gives a man greater satisfaction and sense of fulfillment than a realized sense of importance. Men want recognition. They thrive on it. ... Nothing like this is natural to the woman. If she is aggressive or domineering it is because she has been made so, and that is not good. Two egotists do not easily make a harmonious pair."[9]

As recently as 1966 the Newman Press in Westminster, Maryland, published a translation of the French work by Fathers E. Danniel and B. Oliver, *Woman Is the Glory of Man*; here one learns, with only slight astonishment, that the "entire psychology" of the book's subject "is founded upon the primordial tendency to love," that she manifests "a natural spontaneity toward submission," that she is "more easily subject to illusions," and—surely this is the end—that "Her brain is generally lighter and simpler than man's, which may explain her lesser capacity for deduction."

In a word, as Cardinal Suenen recently put it, "Woman's choice is to be Eve or Mary. Either she ennobles or raises man up . . . or she drags him down with her in her own fall." Significantly, when this was read to an 18-year-old Catholic girl, her immediate response was: "Does this man really exist, or was the statement made in the Middle Ages?"[10] Alas, the answer is yes to both parts of her question.

The spirit of the young lady is at the core of the Church's crisis, and John XXIII, as in *Pacem in Terris* (1963), was bravely confronting it. Thus he said: "Since women are becoming ever more conscious of their human dignity, they will not tolerate being treated as mere material instruments, but demand rights befitting a human person both in domestic and in public life." And, again, even more deeply he added:

Thus in very many human beings the inferiority complex which endured for hundreds and thousands of years is disappearing, while in others there is an attenuation and gradual fading of the corresponding superiority complex which had its roots in social-economic privileges, sex, or political standing.

The male supremacist mythology permeates the literature and history of the United States as completely as that of any other country; what, in a pioneering study, Barbara Welter has called "The Cult of True Womanhood" drenched nineteenth century American writing, written by and for the white middle and upper classes. Woman's virtues were four: piety, purity, submissiveness, and domesticity. As to the first, she was possessed of a "peculiar susceptibility" towards religion; useful, since "God increased the cares and sorrows of woman." Loss of virtue, in the fiction of the time, often led to a loss of mind, so that as Professor Welter writes, "The frequency with which derangement follows loss of virtue suggests the exquisite sensibility of woman, and the possibility that . . . her intellect was geared to her hymen, not her brain." In general, too effective a brain was unwomanly, and, as one best seller said, "the greater the intellectual force, the greater and more fatal the errors into which women fall who wander from the Rock of Salvation. ...."[11] Of all the virtues, "submission was perhaps the most feminine," and this because right-thinking women were "conscious of inferiority." This quality was expected of children, again because their reasoning was deficient, and so it was hoped that women would try to make of their lives "a perpetual childhood" or to "become as little children."

Emerson was certain that woman was "more vulnerable, more infirm, more mortal than man," and it is Hawthorne's Zenobia who, having in mind the marriage night, remarks: "How can she be happy, after discovering that fate has assigned her but one single event, which she must contrive to make the substance of her whole life? A man has his choice of innumerable events."[12]

Education for the woman, therefore, must aim only at producing "a good friend, wife and mother"; it "should be preeminently religious," to quote the views of headmasters of seminaries in New Hampshire and in Ohio. But as late as 1906, so eminent a scientist as E. L. Thorndike of Columbia University, believing that woman's mental capcity was distinctly inferior to that of man—as he put it, man's capacity showed much greater "variability and therefore greater genius capacity"—insisted that while the female might benefit from elementary and high school education, there was no point to the process going any higher.[13]

Just as the Fathers affirmed that a woman who had grasped theology thereby became manly, so one finds Voltaire—far from a Church Father!—remarking of Madame du Chatelet, whose translation of and commentaries upon Newton presented him to the French, "A woman who has translated and illuminated Newton is, in short, a very great man!" And in 1913, Jean Finot thought it worthwhile to tell readers that "women of genius and talent are not necessarily depraved"![14]

On this attitude toward woman, as on sex in general and on reason, Marxism differs fundamentally from the traditional and still dominant positions of religion. Marxism rejects elitism root and branch, whether based upon class, color, national origin, sex, or upon any other criterion. The position is consistent and, I think, has been invariable in the classical writings, in party programs and platforms, and, generally speaking, in practice. On the latter one must add the cautionary note, for Marxists come out of their own social orders, of course, and these have been steeped in the subordination of women, a condition that long antedated capitalism and that certainly is not eliminated quickly with the triumph of socialism. On the basis of repeated personal observation and investigation and rather conscientious study, I assert with some confidence that very significant progress has been achieved in all the states where capitalism has been overthrown in the position of women and in the attitudes held—by men and women—toward the question of women's rights and capacities. Much remains to be accomplished in this sphere, and women living in socialist countries are the first to make this clear; on the other hand a great deal has been accomplished, and this is the more remarkable when one recalls the historical attitude toward and the positions of women in Eastern Europe, in Asia, and in Cuba, where the revolution so far has succeeded.[15]

Certainly the position of Marxism on this question is perfectly clear and stands diametrically opposed to the traditional postures taken by the major religions. It may be briefly summarized by Lenin in the third letter of his "Letters from Afar," written in March 1917 while he was still outside Russia (then in Zurich): "If women are not drawn into public service, into the militia, into political life, if women are not torn out of their stupefying house and kitchen environment, it will be *impossible* to guarantee real freedom, it will be *impossible* to build even democracy, let alone socialism" (Lenin's italics).[16]

This position is envisioned with the special genius that belonged to Walt Whitman, in his "Song of the Broad Axe":

> Where women walk in public processions in
>   the street the same as men,
> Where they enter the public assembly and
>   take places the same as men,
> Where the city of the faithfullest friends stands,
> Where the city of the cleanliness of the sexes stands,

> Where the city of the healthiest fathers stands,
> Where the city of the best-bodied mothers stands,
> There the great city stands.

If this is not Augustine's City of God, perhaps it is close to William Blake's Jerusalem; certainly Whitman's "great city" has the qualities envisioned in the Marxist City of Humanity.

Chapter Eight

Racism and Religion

Francis B. Simkins writes in a well-known work: "The most startling contribution of the Old South to religion was the reconciliation of Christianity with slavery."[1] There is no doubt at all that within the Old South, the dominant tendency was not only to reconcile Christianity with slavery but to insist that Christianity esteemed and supported slavery, particularly the enslavement of colored peoples. The reconciliation of the one with the other was in no way "startling," however; on the contrary, all the Fathers—such as Jerome, Ambrose, Augustine, and Aquinas—had insisted on the propriety of slavery, and this without the added "justification" of racism which was to come some centuries later.

In Christian thought the justification of slavery—which has existed from time immemorial, involving peoples of every clime and origin—took the following forms: slavery as punishment for original sin; slavery as part of the hierarchical character of the world and that character as manifestly part of the Lord's will; slavery as central to societal structure, roughly, to what is now called "law and order"; slavery as inconsequential since it was a temporal and physical state and only the spiritual was of real consequence to the Christian, that is, one was a slave in merely external matters. In any case, Christians were related in a fraternal way whether slave or master, while the non-Christian or pagan "deserved" to be a slave.[2]

Some favorite texts were Noah's cry against Canaan, who had looked upon his nakedness: "Cursed be Canaan, a servant of servants shall he be unto his brethren" (Genesis 9:25); Moses being told on Sinai to purchase slaves from neighboring nations who, being non-Hebraic, "of them shall ye take bondmen for ever" (Leviticus 25:44–46); the author of Ephesus, telling slaves to be obedient "in a singleness of your heart as unto Christ" (Ephesians 6:5–9); and much in Paul, with his exposition of grades and orders and his admonition to slaves not to flee but to serve faithfully their earthly masters (I Corinthians, 12:13–26).

Contrary texts offer contrary views of the idea of the oneness of mankind, that all are of one blood, that in Christ there is neither Christian nor Jew, neither Greek nor Roman, and neither slave nor master. The partiality toward slaves shown at times in the Old Testament and the hostility toward masters; the partiality toward those who hungered and the hostility toward those who were affluent; the hatred of the money-changers and the concern for the meek—such elements could be and were frequently read as meaning that Christ had come to the earth in the form of man and had come for the earth, and that when he spoke of freedom he meant here and now on this earth, and that seeking it here and in reality was doing his work. But those who persisted in so reading the "Good News" generally were treated by the church as the then-church treated him, and from him on to John Brown in the last century and Martin Luther King, Jr. just the other day, it seems.

When German peasants arose for emancipation in the sixteenth century and appealed to Luther that they were acting out Christ's commands, (since he had died to make men free), it was Luther who condemned them as making Christianity entirely of flesh ("*ganz fleishchlich*") and who urged the Princes to put them to the blade and the fire without mercy as the "mad dogs they were."

Speaking of the post-Constantine church on into the Middle Ages, David B. Davis writes:

The Church not only accepted the institution [of slavery], but made every effort to ensure the security of masters in controlling their property. Thus the Canons of the Church reinforced civil law in protecting owners against the loss of slaves to the Church. . . . The Fathers exhorted slaves to obey even the harshest masters, and in A.D. 362 the Council of Gangrae laid anathema on "anyone who under the pretence of godliness should teach a slave to despise his master, or to withdraw himself from his service."[3]

For centuries, of course, popes, bishops, churches, and monasteries themselves owned slaves, missionaries were attached to all the great slave-trading forts and posts in Africa, and care was taken to assure owners and civil authorities that baptism did not offer any grounds for the manumission of a slave. At best, as institutions, churches urged kindness in the treatment of slaves; in general even this was often overlooked in the passion with which the institution was defended.

The churches went along with and helped to establish the justification for modern slavery that, in its origin, was racism. This does not appear in Western civilizations (though there is some evidence of it in early Chinese and Indian civilizations) until the ravishment of Africa, beginning in the fifteenth century. From then to the 1950s, Christian churches—except those created by Afro-Americans themselves—and Jewish temples, with rare exceptions in both cases, have been central expositors and practitioners of racism. Religion made of itself, in fact, the leading apologist for the enslavement of colored peoples (Indian and Afro-American) and the special instrument for the security of such property.

In his diary for 1706 Cotton Mather notes the gift of a slave as a special blessing, "a mighty smile of heaven upon his family." In his *Essays To Do Good*, published four years later, he urged that masters see to the Christian instruction of their slaves, for: "Certainly, they would be the better servants to you, the more faithful, the more honest, the more industrious, and submissive servants to you, for your bringing them into the service of your common Lord." This remained a central theme for church figures for generations thereafter; this, plus the note struck by the Bishop of London in 1727: "Christianity, and the embracing of the Gospel, does not make the least alteration in Civil Property, or in any of the Duties which belong to Civil Relations. . . . The Freedom which Christianity gives is a Freedom from the Bondage of Sin and Satan. . . ."

109

Antonio Vieira, a Jesuit priest in Brazil, offered this message in the seventeenth century, as summarized by David B. Davis:

[He] told Negro slaves that he knew of their wounds and scourgings, their hunger and fatigue and revilings; but if they endured these sufferings with patience, following the example of the blessed Redeemer, they would have the merit as well as the torment of martyrdom. Their bondage might become a new Calvary, but they must not, merely because their labor was hard, shirk their duty.[4]

Special twists were added to old biblical texts; for example, Dr. Samuel Cartwright insisted that the snake in the Garden was "really" the Negro; in fact, the Doctor not only knew that but added that he was indeed "the negro gardener"![5]

Among the most widely distributed sermons meant especially for slaves in eighteenth-century America were those delivered by the Reverend Thomas Bacon of the Protestant Episcopal church of Maryland. He made it clear in the 1740s that the "great general rule" flowing from Christian teaching meant for slaves was "that you are to *do all service for your masters and mistresses, as if you did it for* GOD *Himself.* . . ."[6] While the Bacon sermons were used in the nineteenth century, more popular then were the *Sermons Addressed to Masters and Servants* coming from the Episcopal Bishop William Meade of Virginia. A summary of Bishop Meade's work published some years ago reads:

The slaves here are assured that God has willed that they occupy their lowly position. They are told that unless they perform their allotted tasks well they will suffer eternally in Hell. Specifically, they are warned that the Lord is greatly offended when they are saucy, impudent, stubborn, or sullen. Nor are they to alter their behavior if the owner is cross or mean or cruel; that is the Lord's concern, not theirs and they are to leave the master's punishment to Him.[7]

Much time and ingenuity was spent by the Bishop in explaining away what he called "correction," by which he meant the lash, the paddle, or the club. If it were "deserved" surely one could not complain; if it were not "deserved" perhaps the sufferer had done some wrong earlier for which he had not been punished and now was getting his due. But if all this was not true and one was being

110

"corrected," though he had never done anything meriting it—"a case hardly to be imagined"—why then, "there is this great comfort in it, that if you bear it patiently, and leave your cause in the hands of God, He will reward you for it in heaven, and the punishment you suffer unjustly here shall turn to your exceeding great glory hereafter." As the Alabama Baptist Association resolved in 1850, "intelligent masters with the light of experience before them will regard the communication of sound religious instruction [to their slaves] as the truest economy and the most efficient police and as tending to the greatest utility, with regard to every interest involved."[8]

Dominant opinion and action by the institutional leaders of the Protestant, Roman Catholic, and Jewish religions after Emancipation were as thoroughly racist as before. I. A. Newby is indubitably correct when he writes, ". . . American Protestantism has always discriminated against Negroes. . . ." It is true, also, as Robert M. Miller declared, that there has been an "unhappy correlation between Protestantism and mob violence" directed against black people in the United States.[9]

W. E. B. Du Bois wrote in 1925 that the Roman Catholic church, in both the North and the South, practiced "color separation and discrimination to a degree equalled by no other church in America"; as was his wont he documented this with reference to the realities concerning the personnel in its hierarchy, among priests in the parishes, in Catholic schools of all levels, and in all other church facilities. In terms of racism, David H. Pierce wrote truly when he declared that in "actuality American Jews as a mass have accepted the standards of the Anglo-Saxon. No Southern rabbi has jeopardized his position or his life by running counter to the Klan's dictum that black and white must be forever separate." Pierce added, correctly again, that differing degrees of dissent from this racist pattern appeared among some Jewish "philanthropists, members of radical labor groups and free lance intellectuals."[10] With Jews, for obvious reasons, the degree of dissent was probably greater than with Christians through most of the post–Civil War period; but in all cases exceptions were not wanting, and these based their affirmations and their activities on a radical reading of their religions.

111

Such reading has been common though never dominant; in no area is this more noteworthy than in that relating religion and racism. Certain sects as a whole were suspect by the master class; this was especially true of the Quakers and of the (early) Methodists and, to a lesser degree, of the (early) Baptists. But religious inspiration as such often was a fundamental component in the thinking and acting of white men and women who braved scorn, prison, injury, and death for attacking the slave trade and the institution of slavery. This is true of people like Thomas Clarkson, William Wilberforce, William Lloyd Garrison, Lydia Maria Child, Lucretia Mott, Theodore Weld, the Grimké sisters, Theodore Parker, John Brown, Harriet Beecher Stowe, and others.[11]

In the twentieth century, the established (white) churches in the United States (and elsewhere in the "free" world) continued their racist outlook and practice with no significant break until about nine years after the 1954 decision of the U.S. Supreme Court against segregation. Since then, however, the shift has been mainly verbal; fine-sounding resolutions have abounded, but action to match the language has remained exceptional. Particularly when one bears in mind the colossal real estate, financial, social, political, and psychological power and potential of organized religion in the United States and contrasts this potential for effective action with the relative absence of such action, the failure of religion in the area of combatting racism becomes all the more glaring. Indeed, expressions opposing church action against racism (or any other social activity) are common and still reflect majority opinion within the organized institutional framework.

In addition, of course, positive defense of racism as divine frequently appears from church quarters, not only in South Africa where this is required, but also in the United States where, in its institutional aspects, it is supposed to be unlawful. Thus, in 1968, tens of thousands of copies were circulated of the sermon-tract, "Fusion of the Races, or, A Mongrel American Tomorrow," written by the Reverend Byron M. Wilkinson, pastor of the Hatcher Memorial Baptist Church in Richmond, Virginia. Here one learns: "Homogenized race is called *integration.* Homogenized religion is called *ecumenicism.* Homogenized society is called *communism.*"

112

The Bible, stated this Reverend, "separates everything and everybody. It segregates the sheep from the goats; the believer from the unbeliever; right from wrong; heaven from hell; . . . and race from race."[12]

Senator George S. McGovern, a Democrat from South Dakota, spoke truly when he warned an international conference on racism (sponsored by the World Council of Churches and held in London in May 1969) that, "We had better come to grips with the problem or else the church will become an irrelevant institution. The black man", he added, "is obviously reaching the end of his endurance."[13]

A unique feature of the history of the United States is the history of its Afro-American people. Nothing more clearly reflects this than the history of religion in the United States, for while it has acted predominantly as a bulwark of the status quo, including the slavery and the racism that have characterized that status quo, this clearly was impossible for the religious concepts or practices of those American Christians who were black.

It might be added that while ancient literature (and even the literature of the Middle Ages, though then there were exceptions) shows no hint of condemnation of slavery, such condemnation appeared regularly in the actions of the slaves themselves. Their testimony lay in the suicides, arson, flights, plots, and rebellions that always and everywhere characterized slavery, from the ancient Crimea and Rome, from ancient Egypt and Greece, from medieval Germany and Scotland, from colonial Brazil and South Carolina, to mid-nineteenth-century Cuba and Virginia. Very often the rationalization for such actions, including uprisings, were religious, symbolized above all by the thirty-one-year-old Nat Turner, held in a Virginia jail, wounded, knowing that his comrades had already been executed, himself facing imminent execution, interrogated by a white court-appointed officer, and flinging to that man's demand that Turner admit he was wrong the deathless question: "Was not Christ crucified?"

During the American Revolution the organization of separate churches for black men and women first appeared, in Virginia by 1776 and in Georgia by 1779. These were Baptist churches; among

113

their early leaders were George Liele and Andrew Bryan, who purchased the freedom of his own wife. These separate churches, which served free as well as slave, tended to be urban in the pre–Civil War South and, especially in periods of marked unrest (as in 1800, 1822, and in 1831), they met hostility and even persecution from the master class. As a rule, however, they were viewed benignly, and tended to repay such confidence by urging resignation rather than rebellion. Still, the very fact that they existed and were black-run meant—in a slave and racist society—some element of protest.

In the next decade the free Negro population in the North, especially in Philadelphia where this population was greatest, separated themselves from the white and Jim Crow church. This did not occur until years of protest against a racist Christ had been in vain; then, under the leadership of Richard Allen and Absalom Jones, were founded the African Methodist Episcopal church and the A. M. E. Zion church. As their constitutions made clear, these churches were open to people of all colors, but in fact from their founding the "African" component has been overwhelming. The central point is that these churches, founded by and for black people in protest against racism, constituted a central thread in the history of the church for the Afro-American. And that thread, unlike dominant white churches, was not one of acquiescence in or support for the status quo, but rather objection to and opposition against that status quo. Hence, from the birth of churches for and by black people, the tradition that was dominant in their Christianity was the tradition of concern for life on earth, concern for man here and now; a concentration upon the social duty and function of the church.

This point is not to be exaggerated, for there was the Liele-Bryan tradition, too; and pressures upon the Allen-Jones style of churches in the direction of "respectability" and conformity were powerful and often effective. Nevertheless, the great fact remains that the source and wellspring of much of the Negro church in the United States was protest, and the experiences of black men and women were such as to ever feed and intensify that feature.

Further, of all institutions among Afro-Americans, the one least subject to direct white policing and control (including financial) was the church; this feature, together with the other factors mentioned, tended to make the church and its minister centers of service for the entire surrounding population. In that sense, it is indicative that so many of the greatest figures in black history have been of the church, such as Richard Allen, Peter Williams, Christopher Rush, Samuel R. Ward, Henry Highland Garnet, Alexander Crummell, Henry M. Turner, Alexander Walters, Francis J. Grimké, George Frazier Miller, Martin Luther King, Jr., and Ralph D. Abernathy.

Politicking, fawning, demagoguery, and corruption were not absent from the Afro-American church, for it was a human institution in the midst of an exploitative society; in particular, perhaps, the church connections of many Negro institutions of learning often had a cramping impact. It is this, probably, that helps to account for the emphasis with which W. E. B. Du Bois wrote in his final years that "the Soviet Union does not allow any church of any kind to interfere with education, and religion is not taught in the public schools," which seemed to him to be "the greatest gift of the Russian Revolution to the modern world."[14]

But the main distinguishing feature of the black church was protest. Thus, one should compare the Resolution in 1850 of the Alabama [white] Baptist Church with the Resolution adopted in 1840 by the Tenth Annual Conference of the Western (Pittsburgh) District of the African Methodist Episcopal church:

We, the members of this Conference, are fully satisfied that the principles of the gospel are arrayed against all sin, and that it is the duty of all Christians to use their influence and energies against all systems that rudely trample under foot the claims of justice and the sacred principles of revelation. And, whereas, slavery pollutes the character of the church of God, and makes the Bible a sealed book to thousands of immortal beings—Therefore,

Resolved, on motion, That we will aid, by our prayers, those pious persons whom God has raised up to plead the cause of the dumb, until every fetter shall be broken and all men enjoy the liberty which the gospel proclaims.[15]

115

RACISM AND RELIGION

Frederick Douglass, in one of the great speeches in American history, "The Meaning of July Fourth for the Negro", delivered in Rochester on July 5, 1852, discussed slavery and racism and religion at great length and from many angles. Extracts will suggest his powers of both feeling and analysis. In speaking of the recently enacted Fugitive Slave Law, he says:

I take this law to be one of the grossest infringements of Christian Liberty, and, if the churches and ministers of our country were not stupidly blind, or most wickedly indifferent, they, too, would so regard it. . . .

At the very moment that they are thanking God for the enjoyment of civil and religious liberty, and for the right to worship God according to the dictates of their own consciences, they are utterly silent in respect to a law which robs religion of its chief significance and makes it utterly worthless to a world lying in wickedness. . . . The fact that the church of our country (with fractional exceptions) does not esteem "the Fugitive Slave Law" as a declaration of war against religious liberty, implies that that church regards religion simply as a form of worship, an empty ceremony, and *not* a vital principle, requiring active benevolence, justice, love, and good will towards man. It esteems sacrifice above mercy; psalm-singing above right-doing; solemn meetings above practical righteousness. A worship that can be conducted by persons who refuse to give shelter to the homeless, to give bread to the hungry, clothing to the naked, and who enjoin obedience to a law forbidding these acts of mercy is a curse, not a blessing to mankind.[16]

Douglass continued that the church was not only indifferent—this would be horror enough. But "it actually sides with the oppressors. It has made itself the bulwark of American slavery, and the shield of American slavehunters." "Eloquent Divines," Douglass went on, "have shamelessly given the sanction of religion and the Bible to the whole slave system." In the face of "this horrible blasphemy," said Douglass, "I would say, welcome infidelity! welcome atheism! welcome anything! in preference to the gospel, *as preached by those Divines!*"

These blasphemers, said Douglass—but eleven years out of slavery and with his own flesh and blood still in slavery—produce "a religion for oppressors, tyrants, man-stealers, and *thugs* . . . a religion which favors the rich against the poor; which exalts the

116

proud above the humble . . . which says to the man in chains, *stay there*; and to the oppressor, *oppress on*; . . . a religion which may be professed and enjoyed by all the robbers and oppressors of mankind."

Douglass was not yet through with the American church; as he had said on another occasion, "he who is whipped must cry out." Not only did the church rationalize slavery and support laws that harried the innocent and tormented mothers; it did this though it had the strength—would it but exert it—to bring the damned institution down. The church, said Douglass "is superlatively guilty when viewed in its connection with its ability to abolish slavery."

Let the religious press, the pulpit, the Sunday School, the conference meeting, the great ecclesiastical, missionary, Bible and tract associations of the land array their immense powers against slavery, and slave-holding; and the whole system of crime and blood would be scattered to the winds, and that they do not do this involves them in the most awful responsibility of which the mind can conceive.

More briefly, the man who took the torch from the fallen Douglass asked half a century later in Georgia two questions whose answers are clear; his requestioning again shows the basic posture of black people in the United States toward the Gospel: "who can doubt," Du Bois asked in 1907, "that if Christ came to Georgia today one of His first deeds would be to sit down and take supper with black men, and who can doubt the outcome if He did?"[17]

Six decades later, the Reverend Channing Phillips of the United Christ Church in Washington urged the necessity of the churches fighting racism as a matter of survival; to do this they must leave "the false base of pietism." The Reverend Mr. Phillips indicted "the capitalistic system" that "developed racist ideologies" to support its lust for profits and markets; he denounced resulting priorities that smacked of "insanity," such as building guns rather than fighting hunger, and he affirmed that he was not especially optimistic as far as the established churches were concerned, for they have "a penchant for letting economic factors silence moral requirements." In his view, however, those latter requirements were decisive for a church that was true to its spirit and message, and in being

117

true to this, that church should "shy away from" nothing that may be required for the fulfillment of its message—even, should nothing else be available, said the Reverend Mr. Phillips, "the power of violence."[18]

Marxism's position on racism is unequivocal. Its appearance in the modern world—beginning roughly in the sixteenth century— is related to the appearance and growth of capitalism. As capitalism penetrated the New World, Africa, and India and its environs, it ravished them either for labor power, for raw materials, and/or for markets; at the same time, their possession had significance in diplomatic, military, and political terms insofar as the capitalist nation-states competed among themselves. Justifying this ravishment were the concepts of the pagan as the eternal enemy and the colored one as subhuman or, if human, decisively and immutably inferior to the white. Since these nations already had concepts of elitism and societal gradations basic to their thought patterns, it was not very difficult, given the temptations, to evolve more or less gradually the ideology of racism.[19]

Marx and Engels exhibited their genius nowhere more graphically than in their very early comprehension of the divisiveness of racism and the necessity that this be combatted in the most vigorous and most principled form. Their writings—particularly in connection with slavery, the Civil War, and Reconstruction in the United States; the Irish question and its relationship to social progress, and especially working-class advance, in England; the oppression of the Asian peoples, especially the Indian and Chinese, by Western Europe; and the organic relationship between the rape of Africa, the African slave trade, and the growth of commercial capitalism—provide not only penetrating historical commentary but also incisive social analysis. As one would expect with Lenin —since here one enters the decisive period of monopoly development, worldwide colonialism and imperialism—the concern with racism becomes even more marked and plays a major part in his writings and activities.

Indeed, among the factors producing the historic break with Kautsky, Bernstein, and Plekhanov, racism (and colonialism) is fundamental; it is second only to—and in a sense basically con-

118

nected with—the cleavage over war and internationalism versus nationalism. A tendency to subordinate or to ignore racism has appeared from time to time among those who consider themselves Marxists. Sometimes this was done from the Left, as it were, for example, in Debs's insistence that the only meaningful conflict was that between worker and boss, and that insofar as the black people were workers they had a significant tie to socialism, but in terms of their particular oppression stemming from the fact that they were black and in the United States Debs chose to be silent. Sometimes this came from the Right—and was a pure kind of opportunism, even to the point of blatant and explicit racism—as with Victor Berger. More often this showed itself in less open forms: in compromise, keeping quiet, or in demeaning the basic consequence of racism.[20]

No matter what the guise, Marxism rejects all positions that compromise in any way with racism; it affirms the basic connection between racism and capitalism (and especially imperialism); sees it as a ruling-class instrument for furthering economic exploitation, weakening working-class unity, vitiating democratic strength, and bolstering forces of reaction—particularly, in the present period, fascist forces. This does not mean that the Marxist views racism as a simple matter; on the contrary, it is infinitely complex in its manifestations and powerful in its persisting capacities. But Marxism does not view it as a "dilemma"; it does not view it, in origin, as a moral or psychological problem (though it has strong overtones of both). It insists that its extirpation requires the elimination of the private ownership of the means of production and production conducted on that basis for purposes of individual appropriation of profits. This elimination does not automatically end racism, but it does lay the groundwork for such an end.

As in the case of overcoming male supremacy, socialist societies have achieved magnificent results in the struggle against racism. In such societies, racism is generally exceptional rather than the rule, and a constant educational and practical campaign is maintained against it. There have been failures and even relapses in such societies, but these are rare and have not altered the main line of development toward making racism extinct and evolving a population that considers racism and racist practices barbaric. Again, when one considers that socialism has appeared in many societies where racism was long established and virulent—as in czarist Russia, old Poland, Hungary, and Rumania—the achievements are all the more notable. In Cuba, where racism took substantially the same form as in the United States (though with less intensity) its socialist society has significantly succeeded in eliminating it.[21]

Chapter Nine

Life, Death, and Religion

Roger Garaudy, a philosopher and a member of France's Communist party, when asked what he thought Marxism might have to gain from conversations with Christians, replied that Christianity still raised the same questions it had considered for many years. Its answers, he believed, "are out of date," but raising questions was an important service; the particular question Garaudy cited was "the problem of death." He went on to say that he had been "invited to a colloquium with the Dominicans on this question" and that, as a Marxist, "I arrive with empty hands."[1] As a Marxist, I do not understand Garaudy's feeling of emptiness on this particular question. Some believe that death offers mankind two possible responses: hope or despair. Others feel that death mirrors the absurdity of life. These views do not exhaust the possible alternatives.

One may achieve a kind of hope through concepts of either resurrection or immortality, or—as has happened in a rather careless and little-analyzed way—through a concept that combines resurrection with immortality. This, however, has led to deprecation of the consequence of this life. In Calvin's words, ". . . in comparison with the immortality to come, let us despise life and long to renounce it."[2] This lends itself to the extension of "pie in the sky"; resignation to the momentary experience endured in this life helping to assure eternal bliss in the next one. It induces not only such a personal reaction but also a generalized view of religion as something to be kept out of any concern with this world; from this naturally follows the view that resents any concern with social problems as anachronistic for a church, even as almost blasphemous.

Increasingly, as the untenable character of what Corliss Lamont called *The Illusion of Immortality* has become more and more persuasive, hope has given way to despair.[3] William James observed over fifty years ago that "Religion, in fact, for the great majority of our own race, *means* immortality and nothing else. God is the producer of immortality." But today, writes Milton Gatch, "we have lost our faith in the doctrine of immortality". Combining the opinions of James and Gatch will help to pinpoint one focus of religion's crisis.[4] An extreme form of despair—common for those who, having been religious, now find God dead—is to insist that life itself is simply absurd; one aspect of a generalized view of the meaninglessness of existence is to hold that since life terminates with death, the whole process is absurd.

However, there are other ways of viewing and evaluating death. There were at least two traditions among the ancient Greeks, for example: one taught a kind of immortality of the soul, whereas the other held to the immortality of the memory of the one who had died. The latter depended upon the concept of service for one's people; this service induced memory, and that memory was, in fact, immortality. The Hebrew tradition did not hold to immortality of the soul; in line with its overwhelming concern with His chosen people, it emphasized the destiny of that people, and the point of immortality lay in one's contribution to the working out of that divine destiny. In that sense—in the sense of service to those left behind—the Hebrew tradition was akin to one of those that was strong among the Greeks.

The early teachings of Christianity in the New Testament,—and found also in the Old Testament—present death not as an active condition in itself but rather as a conclusion, with the persistence of mankind and memory among the living being the form of one's immortality. The original emphasis of both the Hebrew and the

Christian was upon this world; with the transformation of Christianity into ultimate concern for the next world, the emphasis of Christian doctrine turned to a theology of rewards and punishments. Today, with the concept of immortality, understood as either bodily resurrection or eternal existence of soul (or both), increasingly difficult to maintain and therefore disappearing, a theology based upon it is less and less adequate.

A fourth view of death neither hopeful, nor despairing, nor affirming absurdity—namely, showing a kind of indifference to it— is sometimes ascribed to the Communist (this is supposed to reflect his robot-like nature). For example, in *Darkness At Noon*, Arthur Koestler writes that "In the Party death was no mystery, it had no romantic aspect. . . . The act of dying in itself was a technical detail, with no claim to interest. . . ." It may have been possible to ignore this absurdity except that it has been offered to illustrate the view of death held "in politically orthodox circles in Eastern Europe."[5] Simply from the viewpoint of methodology, to offer as the view of death held by numerous—if "orthodox"—circles something pronounced by a character in a novel whose theme is to justify the author's attacking such "circles" would seem to be, if not quite unfair, surely rather unusual!

A Marxist views death not as an absurdity, not as a source of hope, not as a source of despair, and not as a matter of indifference. He views death as implicit in all life, as life's termination, as a necessity if the life cycle is to continue. He views it as postponable, and notes with delight that the average longevity of man has risen where conditions of living have improved. But the process of living is itself a process of renewal and of decay, and at a point in each individual decay finally overcomes renewal; aging appears and terminates in death.[6] For the Marxist this life is the only one there is; why should this not enhance its preciousness and induce a desire to make the most of it rather than induce despair? For the Marxist life is not individual and therefore one follows false paths if he seeks individual salvation, no matter how he defines salvation. Death's finality enhances life's value, intensifies its challenge.

The Marxist would find precious little to object to in Benjamin Franklin's belief, in his *Autobiography*, "that the most acceptable service of God was the doing of good to men." We are of the past and in the present, and we are of the social whole; without this locus of time and place and this development out of history we are not conceivable. In our time and place and out of the whole that bore us and shaped us we are to make our contribution, do our work, end some misery, and provide some joy, and thus contribute to making life better or fuller or easier or nobler. If we do, we live well, and will live on in what others do, hopefully more successfully, with the greater success possibly depending to some degree upon what we did. This influence and continuity mean immortality to the Marxist. No blow for human freedom is ever wholly lost; deliver such blows while one lives and the space and air one consumed will have been well used. Meanwhile, Communists, too, have children—even those in "politically orthodox circles in Eastern Europe"!—and they wish for them a world without war, without poverty, without hunger, without racism, and without the humiliation of people. To help bequeath this to their children moves them, too—as others who have children—and if they do anything at all to help this process they will, Marxists believe, have earned immortality.

Earlier I have cited Gatch somewhat critically; however, I can agree warmly with the conclusion of his work. He finds that "literally conceived, the idea of an afterlife has no place, makes no sense, and is inconsistent within the framework of the contemporary world-picture. . . . Christians should not try to force themselves to conceive of what is inconceivable in their world." "The solution," he believes, "lies not in a new or revived ideological formulation but in an attitude toward death which makes clear the importance of being involved in the world among men who are trying to fulfill the promise of a vision of the world transformed."[7] There is such an attitude and it is the Marxist one; that it is not exclusively Marxist is shown by the fact of Gatch's recommendation. So, too, it represents the end view of the humanism in Corliss Lamont, who concludes his volume on the problem of death by writing that while we do live, "We can make our actions count and endow our days on earth with a scope and a meaning that the finality of death cannot defeat." And it cannot defeat it because "We can contribute our unique quality to the ongoing development of the nation and humanity; give of our best to the continuing affirmation of life on behalf of the greater glory of man."[8]

Certainly, for the Marxist, to speak of one who has died is to speak of the life he or she led; in doing so, it is not unusual at all to find the affirmation of death overcome. For example, Lenin writes of a Russian worker, Ivan Vasilyevich Babushkin, killed by the Czar's forces during the 1905 Revolution: ". . . in dying, he knew that the cause to which he had devoted his life would not die, that it would be continued by tens, hundreds of thousands, millions of other hands, that other working-class comrades would die for the same cause, that they would fight until they were victorious."[9]

In a personal sense, one may view death as final rest, as prolonged sleep well earned after intense and long labors. The Russian biologist Ilya Metchnikoff projected the idea of what he called "orthobiosis," which he defined as "the development of human life so that it passes through a long period of old age in active and vigorous health leading to the final period in which there shall be present a sense of satiety of life and a wish for death."[10] There are two lines in a poem by the then 74-year-old Walter Savage Landor that evoke this:

> I warmed both hands before the fire of life;
> It sinks, and I am ready to depart.[11]

Of no one is this process and this willingness to finally call it off clearer than of W. E. B. Du Bois, who died in 1963 at the age of 95. Du Bois, who for most of his adult life believed in socialism and in his final years chose to become a Communist, prepared, in his characteristically careful manner, a final testament to be read at his funeral. His statement is redolent of the Old Testament, with its repeated reference to death as "sleep" and its sense of the continuity of the human drama.

It is much more difficult in theory than actually to say the last good-bye to one's loved ones and friends and to all familiar things of this life.

I am going to take a long, deep and endless sleep. This is not a punishment but a privilege to which I looked forward for years.

I have loved my work, I have loved people and my play, but always I have been uplifted by the thought that what I have done ill or never finished

125

can now be handed on to others for endless days to be finished, perhaps better than I could have done.

And that peace will be my applause.

One thing alone I charge you. As you live, believe in life. Always human beings will live and progress to greater, broader and fuller life.

The only possible death is to lose belief in this truth simply because the great end comes slowly, because time is long.

Good-bye.[12]

It is relevant to recall that Engels, in his eulogy at the graveside of Marx in March 1883, began by commenting that his great friend had "peacefully gone to sleep—but for ever." Engels concluded by observing that Marx had earned the hatred of ruling classes throughout the world, but that "he died beloved, revered and mourned by millions of revolutionary fellow workers." What he had discovered and built would live through those workers; therefore, Engels closed: "His name will endure through the ages, and so also will his work!"[13] There is more reason today than when Engels uttered it to believe in the accuracy of his prediction.

Present in the remarks of Lenin, Du Bois, and Engels—and in the humanism illustrated by Gatch and Lamont—is an adherence to the concept of progress. Such adherence is related not only to one's estimate of humankind, which has been spoken of earlier, but also to one's view of the problem of evil and the efficacy of human struggle.

Marxism is wedded to the concept of progress: the enhancement of productivity, the rationalization of distribution, the elimination of alienation, the extirpation of all forms of debasement, and the flowering of creativity. The charge is commonly made that while Marxism seeks and believes in such progress, its approach guarantees failure. Thus, typically, Samuel Hugo Berman writes:

> The aim of Marxism is the reorganization of the social order, not the renewal of the human spirit. It concentrates on externals to the total neglect of inner factors: It seeks to change man by changing the regime instead of seeking to change the regime by changing man. All attempts to transform human life through the introduction of a new social order are doomed to failure if they do not begin with what must come first: the living human being.[14]

126

Bergman's presentation represents the characteristic caricature of Marxism. Marxism does not function disjointly and cannot operate—and be Marxism—in a separated, mechanical fashion, such as by trying to alter externals in the hope that this will effect internals. First, in Marxism there is not a neat separation between the external and the internal, for they are conjoined and interpenetrating and mutually influential. Second, the effort to change the social order depends upon the work and participation and thought and muscle and sacrifice of human beings; in the course of such effort and thought they are themselves changed. If they were not themselves changed, they would be dead; and in their own change they help to change the social order, and the altered social order in turn expedites change in human beings, change in what they think and how they behave.

It was not long ago that it was considered necessary that workers labor twelve or fourteen hours a day, six or seven days a week for the good of their souls; otherwise being poor (that is, workers) and therefore assumed to be deficient, the absence of work would only induce debauchery and greater suffering. It was also not long ago that it was assumed that the children of the poor must work, and work very hard, as soon as they physically could; this was good for their souls and necessary for the functioning of the social order. It was not long ago that all women were considered mentally deficient when compared to men, and that therefore their stations in life had to be subordinate and fixed, else civilization would disintegrate. It was not long ago that black people were thought to be fit only for slavery, that they were in fact created to be the slaves of the superior white folk, and that if this natural and divine order were disturbed due to the fanatical agitation of deluded wretches, civilization would crumble. It is widely held today, in certain civilizations, that war is natural, that it comes from man's innate aggressiveness, and/or that it reflects God's judgment on a sinful mankind as well as His way to control population growth.

To the extent that the preceding concepts have been relegated to museums, it has resulted from changing social orders that could be changed only by human struggle, and such struggle and such

127

change—together, interlocked—finally produced changed "common sense."

The tendency in Western—that is, imperialist—civilizations to repudiate reason and to deny progress, to see *The Human Mind At The End of Its Tether* (the title of H. G. Wells's final book), reflects the obsolescence of the material base of those civilizations; its political image is fascism.[15]

Marxism does not see the existence of evil as reflecting God's punishment or warning or testing or His inexplicable quality. Marxism sees history in its dynamic essence as reflecting class struggle and adopts a partisan position toward such struggle. It does this in terms of the struggles of past epochs when, for example, it favored Lincoln over Jefferson Davis and the Commune over its opponents. And it does this in terms of the present, when it favors socialism over imperialism, national liberation over colonialism, egalitarianism over racism, and working-class organization and struggle over capitalist efforts at suppression, compromise, or corruption.

Hence, from a theoretical viewpoint, so colossal an evil as fascism in general or Auschwitz in particular does not immobilize the Marxist and does not disorient him. It does not destroy his faith in a people having a covenant with God, for he knows no such people; it does not convince him that God has decided to ignore this world, for he knows no such God.[16] It tells him rather of what a reactionary ruling class is capable and for what one must prepare and against what one must battle. It does not convince the Marxist of life's absurdity, for neither the coming nor the defeat of fascism represented absurdity in any possible definition of the term. Nor does it persuade the Marxist—as it seems to have persuaded the author of *After the Fall*—that we are all guilty, inmates and guards alike in the Auschwitzes that "we all build." We know who built the Auschwitzes—all those fine gentlemen of the banks and the munitions works; and we know who profited from them—all those fine gentlemen with their electrical works and their chemical plants. And we know who survived and who fought and who dealt to fascism and all its Auschwitzes the most telling blows; we know these were men and women of hope and conviction and that certainly neither least nor last among them were the Marxists.

128

Thus, to the Marxist, evil is specific and explicable, and the struggle against it gives meaning to life. And that struggle in the past has often been successful, so that while there is much that is ignoble in human history there is also much that is noble. (This is true also of the present.) There is every reason, then, to believe that there will be a future—given the will and the endurance and the effort—and that it will be a good one.

Berdyaev held that it was Christianity, as he defined it, that alone gave meaning to life and made it possible to accept its burdens; "this is what Christianity does," he wrote in *The Destiny of Man*, "and it alone." On this basis, he held, "man can go through the most terrible sufferings." It is certain that men and women have done so and have had as their support their Christianity (or, in other cases, some other religion, and Berdyaev's ignoring of those others is as provincial as his ignoring of Marxism).

In fact, in the supreme testing, as at Auschwitz, those who were Christian and those who were Jewish and those who were not religious, and those who were Communist and those who were Socialist and those who were not political often did stand together; that was, indeed, the character of the Resistance, and in that Resistance surely none will deny that Communists were not among the last to join or the first to leave.

One of the supreme moments of such humanistic unity—triumphant at the time but destined for defeat, though a defeat that will not last forever—was in November 1936, when the fascist forces of Franco—many of them, of course, non-Spanish—penetrated Madrid's outskirts. The defenders were outnumbered and very much outgunned; the fascist planes, tanks, and artillery had finally reduced the defenders' ranks by two-thirds when an appeal from the Government, representing Communists, Socialists, Republicans, Christians, and atheists, came over the radio. "People of Madrid," said the appeal:

> History has presented you in this hour with the great mission of rising up before the world as the obelisk of Liberty. You will tell the world how to be worthy of so exalted a destiny. . . . People of Spain! Put your eyes, your will, your fists at the service of Madrid. Accompany your brothers with faith, with courage, send your possessions, and if you have nothing

else, offer us your prayers. Here in Madrid is the universal frontier that separates Liberty and Slavery. It is here in Madrid that two incompatible civilizations undertake their great struggle: love against hate; peace against war; the fraternity of Christ against the tyranny of the Church. . . . And on the pages of history, Man will engrave an immense heart. This is Madrid. It fought for Spain, for Humanity, for Justice, and with the mantle of its blood sheltered all the men of the world. Madrid! Madrid![17]

Again, in Madrid and in all Spain, the unity of people defending life is growing; evil is being overcome; and on the anvil of agony, progress is being hammered into shape.

Chapter Ten

Marxism, Religion, and Revolution

1

In the summer of 1850, an antislavery convention was meeting in Salem, Ohio. In the pre–Civil War era, abolitionists always faced great difficulties, but at that moment they confronted a particular crisis brought on by the recent passage of the Fugitive Slave Act. Frederick Douglass, himself having fled slavery but a few years earlier, offered the opinion that in the face of the latest atrocity, "There is no longer any hope for justice other than bloody rebellion. Slavery must end in blood." Sitting in the front row was another former slave known as Sojourner Truth. As Douglass finished speaking she rose, pointed a finger at him, and, in a loud voice, demanded: "Frederick, is God dead?" "No," came the reply, "and because God is not dead, slavery can end only in blood."

Alas, as the next decade proved, Douglass was right, and blood drenched the South like water. But relevant as all this is to contemporary problems and events, I call it to mind here because of what it says about God. To one who loved Him, it seemed unthinkable that He would allow blood to drown slavery; another thought He would. This disagreement was deep, but not fundamental, for both Douglass and Truth agreed as to the essential nature—as well as the reality—of God; both agreed that while tactical matters were controversial, strategic considerations were certain. That is, slavery was oppressive and therefore unjust; that oppression was offensive to the Lord was unquestionable, and therefore that He would end it was indubitable.

For those committed to such ends and holding fast to faith, God's death is unthinkable and unbearable; hence, the former slave woman puts the rhetorical question and the former slave man never doubts the answer. A generation later in Germany, the philosopher of despair asks not a question, but in his parable, *The Gay Science*, Nietzsche's madman tells his mocking audience that God is dead, that "we have killed him," and the crowd is amused rather than shocked for, really, they had known it all the time.

As the atrocities of the twentieth century—from Verdun to Guernica to Auschwitz to Hiroshima to yesterday's tonnage dropped upon Vietnam—make those of the nineteenth century seem like almost child's play, they are no longer madmen who seriously raise Sojourner Truth's question. Indeed, the "death of God" literature of the past seven or eight years has reached such flood proportions that there are already two quite distinct anthologies devoted only to this outpouring—those edited by Bernard Ramm in 1965 and by Jackson Ice and John Carey in 1967.

I think one of the contrasting features marking this literature is that the Catholic emphasis suggests the death or, at least, the irrelevance of the present church, while the Protestant emphasis suggests the irrelevance (or disappearance) of God. Regardless, surely such literature reflects profound religious and therefore societal crisis. Today, with all the promises that characterized neoconservatism— the American Century, People's Capitalism, the End of Ideology, and so on—lying about broken where not forgotten, it is not only Communist devils who speak of a crisis society, of basic malfunctioning, of profound structural corrosion. Today the contradictions and antagonisms are so acute that James Reston, managing editor of the *New York Times*, writes in those terms and the chairman of the Senate Foreign Relations Committee, in a speech before the American Bar Association, says: "The Great Society has become the sick society."[1]

Turning more directly to the matter at hand, the literature assumes the crisis in religion and tries to explain and perhaps alleviate it. Typical of such an assumption, for example, is the very able work by Herbert W. Richardson,—*Toward an American Theology*. Here we read: "The matrix of meaning itself has broken down. For this reason, the crisis in religion today is accompanied by concomitant crises in philosophy, politics, economics, education, art, family life, and so forth." Richardson suggests that ". . . the crisis in modern religion does not arise primarily from intrareligious conflicts (as in the 16th century) nor from a conflict between religion and science (as in the 19th century), but arises directly from the deterioration of religion itself."[2]

Richardson's description is accurate but explanation is lacking. To see crisis in religion as the result of intrareligious conflict reveals little, for one immediately wishes to know the source of such conflict; to see a later cause of such crisis as the conflict between religion and science does not explain the development of the latter nor why the two necessarily collided; and to affirm that today's crisis in religion is due to a deterioration in religion seems inadequate, for to speak of religion's deterioration is to speak of religion's crisis. Synonyms may help elucidate character but they do not illuminate cause.

Where religion is now in admitted crisis, the social order itself is in crisis. It seems to have been in chronic and general crisis since at least World War I and the Bolshevik Revolution. With that general crisis and with the Revolution that marks it—and that has since, in various forms, encompassed one-third of the globe—we have entered, I suggest, the post-religious phase of human history; with greater confidence, I agree with those who say that we have entered the post-Constantine era of Christian history.

The Italian scholar, Vittorio Lanternari, in his study of what he calls "modern messianic cults," sees their appearance as reflections of the drive for liberation from colonialism; in this sense, he writes, "they provide one of the most startling demonstrations of the close tie between religious life and secular, political, and cultural life." The cults represent so many "cries for freedom" that they constitute an "indictment of Western civilization." He adds that these cults, in having such origins, are identical with the origins of all the great religions—Buddhism, Taoism, Judaism, Islam, and Christianity. Each, he reminds us, "began as a prophetic movement of renewal stimulated by certain given cultural and social conditions in a time of crisis"; "the striving for religious renewal and liberation arises from the rebellion of the masses against the existing official cults imposed by a ruling caste."[3]

As observed earlier, Engels himself points several times to the "notable points of resemblance" between early Christianity and the working-class movements of modern history; he notes that the "essential feature" of Christianity at its beginning was its partisanship toward the poor, the despised, the enslaved, and the oppressed—a partisanship that Engels writes, "reverses the previous world order."

Early Christianity, as befits its revolutionary character and composition, denounced the ruling gods and so was called atheist, excoriated the secular powers and so was called seditious, upbraided the rich and so was called deluded, pointed to private property and the accumulation of profit and its twin, covetousness, as the chief source of evil, and so was called a dangerous madness to be extirpated from the earth.[4]

Here is the record of one early Christian death, that of Maximilian, near Carthage in the year 295. Maximilian, of an age for army service, is brought before the authorities to be measured and conscripted. But he says, "I cannot serve: I cannot do wrong; I am a Christian." The authorities plead with him and demand of his father, "Who has put these ideas into his head?" Maximilian replies that it is "my conscience" that speaks. The proconsul pleads with the father, "Give him some advice!" The father answers: "He is old enough to know his duty." The proconsul pleads yet again; he says, "Think of your youth and become a soldier. It is a fine life for a young man!" He points out that others who call themselves Christians serve in the army; "That is their business," replies the stubborn one, "I only know I am a Christian and I cannot do wrong."

The official persists: "But those who serve—what wrong do they do?" Such matters are beyond argument for Maximilian; he simply replies: "You know very well what they do."

From arguments to threats: "Come on, now, be a soldier! If you refuse military service, you will die." Maximilian refuses still, and is sentenced "to die by the sword." The record states: "He was twenty-one years old, three months and eighteen days." On the way to his execution, Maximilian urges that the suit prepared for his army service be given, with his compliments, to the executioner. A woman named Pomeia was permitted to take his body and bury it; "twelve days later she too died." The father held firm and gloried in the strength of his Maximilian.[5]

The story of Maximilian rings again in the affirmation of the nine Christian men and women—priests and laymen—who in May 1968 at Catonsville, Maryland, announced that they were burning the draft records of that community with napalm. As they said, they "take the Christian gospel seriously"; they, therefore, indicted the hierarchies of all religions in the United States for being "racist, guilty of complicity in war, and hostile to the poor." They were "appalled by the ruse of the American ruling class invoking pleas for 'law and order' to mask and perpetuate injustice." They closed: "We have pleaded, spoken, marched, and nursed the victims of their injustice. Now this injustice must be faced, and this we intend to do, with whatever strength of mind, body, and grace that God will give us. May He have mercy on our nation."[6]

The post-Constantine history of Christianity is an extraordinary one of success and of "success." The results of the latter, certainly in its institutional aspects, seem to have been summarized accurately by a group of worker-priests in France in their collective letter sent in the summer of 1964 to the Ecumenical Council. "The Church," they wrote,

appears to be an economic, political and cultural *power* which flourishes well under the capitalist system. In those countries where land is the chief source of wealth, the Church possesses enormous riches. It has an enormous personnel and rich institutions, owns splendid buildings. Its economic future is guaranteed by large bank deposits and stocks and bonds which are wisely administered and derive profit from the exploitation of

135

labor. The Church is on good terms with capitalist governments and even with fascist governments, and its leaders are considered among the important people of this world.

Does the Church not therefore defend that social system which permits it to live and flourish?[7]

The fact is, indeed, that the Vatican is the largest single stockholder in the world. Its securities have a value of from five to six billion dollars; its realizable assets equal the gold and foreign exchange reserves of France. Consequential is the fact that the wealth of the modern Vatican was founded upon the Lateran Treaty signed between it and Mussolini in 1929; by that treaty, Vatican City was created, the distribution of Protestant Bibles in Italy was forbidden, Catholicism was declared to be the fascist state's official religion, and instruction in it became compulsory in all Italian schools. Furthermore, as restitution for the Vatican's loss of temporal powers, Mussolini granted it ninety million dollars and agreed that the state would pay the salaries of all priests upon Italian soil (the latter is still done; about 30,000 priests in Italy receive an average annual salary of about $550 from the state). The Vatican's holdings inside Italy include major investments in gas, telephone, food, mines, munitions, shipping, banks, insurance companies, credit corporations, and so on.[8]

Such wealth is not confined to the Vatican, of course. Thus, very large blocs of stock in the Republic and National steel corporations and in the Boeing, Lockheed, Curtiss-Wright, and Douglas aircraft corporations are held by the Jesuit order; it also holds substantial shares in the Di Giorgio Fruit Company, which operates in California, Florida, and Central America, and owns its own fleet of ships. The assets of the Knights of Columbus include the land under Yankee Stadium, several department stores, and a steel tube factory; while a Protestant church in Akron, Ohio, owns a shopping center, an apartment building, an electronics firm, a plastic company, and the Real Form Girdle Company. Protestant churches in Bloomington, Illinois, own the luxury Biltmore Hotel in Dayton, Ohio; while Loyola University in New Orleans is the owner of that city's largest radio-television station.[9]

The Mormon church—whose estimated income is one million

dollars a day—owns the major television station in Salt Lake City, and possesses considerable interest in several newspapers, two life insurance companies, the largest department store in Salt Lake City, two hotels, a trucking company, a pineapple plantation, three large ranches, six hundred farms, forty mills and assorted factories, a sugar company, and a sugar plantation. Through the Deseret Management Company, the Mormon church owns radio stations in Kansas City, Missouri, and in New York City, and a radio-television station in Seattle; it partially controls radio-television stations in Boise and Idaho Falls, Idaho. It also has a five per cent interest (about twenty million dollars) in the *Los Angeles Times*.[10]

Being specifically exempted from the 1950 revision of the Federal tax laws that required secular nonprofit organizations to pay corporate profit taxes on their "unrelated business income," churches have become aggressive business owners and operators and, especially with the so-called "lease-back" technique, have piled money upon money, based on the unique tax advantage, while gaining control of corporations. Testifying before the House Ways and Means Committee in February 1969, Mortimer M. Caplan, former Commissioner of Internal Revenue, stated: "a number of churches have entered into active and aggressive commercial endeavors. One, for example, has become a wholesale distributor of popular phonograph records. Another has acquired at least seven sportswear and clothing manufacturing businesses."[11]

There is no requirement and no practice of revealing financial holdings by churches, and so totals are only guesses; how wide the margin of error may be is indicated in Harvey Cox's report that "In the United States today it has been estimated that the church's assets are worth somewhere between fifty and one hundred *billion* dollars." He adds: "Over 99 percent of this money is now invested with no reference whatsoever to the social purpose such investments serve or do not serve."[12]

Perhaps even more consequential than these direct financial bonds to Mammon is the nature of the laymen whose influence, especially in the United States, has long been decisive in religious establishments. As Alfred Blake writes, normally "the parish governing board (by whatever name it is known) [is] heavily peopled with representatives of the town's business and professional com-munity—ideally, perhaps, a banker; a lawyer; a doctor or dentist; a real estate man; and a corporation executive or two."[13]

The data offered in the preceding paragraphs indicate something of the churches' "success"; they make more comprehensible the sources of the charges leveled against those churches by such pas-sionately practicing Christians as the Catonsville Nine. With mounting taxes and intensifying social crises it is proper to remark that a not altogether dissimilar situation was consequential in bring-ing about the Reformation. Major church bodies and organizations have been reflecting an awareness of this anomaly; they range from the National Federation of Priests Councils (which counts 38,000 priest members out of a total number of 60,000 American priests) to the United Presbyterian Church in the U.S.A., which at its 175th General Assembly (1963) resolved that "the church should know that it renders its witness ambiguous by its continual acceptance of special privileges from the state in the form of tax exemptions," and therefore urged a repeal of the exemption of religious institutions from the tax on profits levied upon businesses unrelated to the proper functions of a church.[14]

The point is that increasingly Christians are saying, to quote the title of Father Robert Adolfs' book, that the church is *The Grave of God*; that is, because they are devout, they are pleading for and working for change—some more and some less fundamental, as their views may differ, but certainly for change. In making these challenges, these devout rebels reflect profound and positive tradi-tions in Christianity, which appear not only in the pre-Constantine phase but also in the centuries thereafter. The turmoil is more intense and more fundamental, perhaps, than in the past; this is as it should be, for the problems and the opportunities are unprece-dented.

One has the tradition of the religiously inspired mass rebellions of the fourteenth, fifteenth, and sixteenth centuries in England, Bohemia, and Germany, with the words and activities of Wycliffe, Huss, Prokop, Münzer, Winstanley, and Ball, and in the sixteenth and seventeenth centuries the great dreams of More and Cam-panella. And some, honored while they lived and influential within

138

the church while they lived, also reflected this egalitarian and com-munistic tradition. Notable in this regard was Ambrose (d. 397), bishop of Milan. In many respects as other-worldly as the most intense traditionalist might desire, he nevertheless demanded jus-tice on earth and asserted that such justice could not appear as long as the private possession of the world's goods prevailed. To seek private profit is to attack public interest, to be rich is to flaunt sin, and both violate the "essential nature of justice." "For so long as we eagerly strive to increase our riches, to accumulate money, to occupy lands as our possessions, to be distinguished for our wealth, we put away from us the essential nature of justice and lose the spirit of common beneficence."

Arthur O. Lovejoy, whose study has rescued this aspect of Am-brose's thought, concludes his exposition with these words:

> The most significant fact concerning this side of the teaching of St. Ambrose is that so little came of it. The most powerful and popular figure in the Latin Church through two critical decades, he played a large part in determining the direction which it was to take in theology, in its ec-clesiastical polity, its liturgy, and its relations to the secular authority. But his preaching of a virtually equalitarian and communistic ideal of a Chris-tian society has no effect commensurate with its earnestness and elo-quence. To the reflective historian, this negative fact calls for an attempt at explanation; but such an attempt would require a long discussion upon which I shall not enter here.[15]

Lovejoy's restraint was unfortunate; without "a long discussion," one may offer the opinion that the equalitarian and communistic side of Ambrose—and not only of him!—has been neglected be-cause of the considerations brought forward by the worker-priests in our time.

Still, there is a thread—a red thread, no doubt—that runs through the history and teaching of many religions and not least that of Christianity. It appears in the actions and writings of those already mentioned, and in the Christianity of a Nat Turner, a John Brown, a Dorothy Day, and increasingly in personalities not associated with the marked radicalism such names suggest.

The Reverend Anthony Towne, writing on "Revolution and the Marks of Baptism," announced that he wished to "seize the bull by the horns," and that Americans in particular had better "reconsider the rights of property, which infect the whole [U.S.] Constitution, and acknowledge that property does not, in fact, have any rights."[16] Archbishop Helder Camara of Brazil warns: "Woe be to all Christians if the lowly become convinced that the Church has abandoned them in this dark hour. They cannot but believe that religion is indeed the opium of the people and Christianity an ally of privilege and exploitation."[17] The Reverend Tissa Belasuriya, writing from Ceylon, makes his warning global. In the Catholic quarterly *Cross Currents*, he denounces the system of capitalism as having resulted in what he calls "world apartheid," and continues:

> The purely atomistic, capitalistic principle that regulates world trade today is basically unjust, and more equitable and effective solutions must be found on the principle of human solidarity. This is not a demand for alms, but an exigency of international social justice. Otherwise it is at present difficult to reverse the process by which poor nations become relatively poorer and the rich nations richer.[18]

Somewhere between 30 and 40 per cent of all professing (not necessarily practicing) Catholics in the world live in Latin America; 93 per cent of its total population profess Catholicism, the proportion varying from a little over 70 per cent in Haiti to about 98 per cent in El Salvador. In Latin America there are approximately 40,000 priests, though a high—and increasing—percentage (especially among the hierarchy) are not of Latin American origin themselves. Projecting present population trends, it is clear that by the year 2000 every other Roman Catholic in the world will be a Latin American. Here, then, one has an area of decisive significance in terms of religion; no one doubts the revolutionary conditions present in Latin America and the vast significance therein of Marxism. Therefore, Latin America provides an excellent case study of the relationships between Marxism and religion, and revolution.

Historically the church has been a basic power throughout the history of Latin America, both before and since independence. In terms of education, ideology, land control, political domination, and wealth, nothing rivals the Roman Catholic church—except the Yankee dollar, and the two have been and are deeply intertwined. Nevertheless, neither in the past and certainly not in the present

140

has the church been monolithic; its institutional weight has been overwhelmingly on the side of the status quo, but significant opposition to such an alignment has always been present among the faithful, and priests like Las Casas, Hidalgo, Morelos, Camilo Henriquez, José Simon Canas, and Medina have helped to develop humanistic and even revolutionary traditions. Today such figures and forces within the church in Latin America are legion, and represent significant threats not only to the institution as such but to the governments and social systems involved—and to the Washington colossus whose worries and preparations mount.

The exploitation and oppression of the two hundred and fifty million Latin Americans have been documented so extensively that little need be said here: it is perhaps sufficient to note that in several countries the per capita yearly income averages $100, and that overall illiteracy averages about 50 per cent. Latin America is normally referred to in the American press as part of the underdeveloped world; the phrase is misleading, however, for Latin America has been overexploited and therefore is underdeveloped. Hence the Economic Commission for Latin America noted that private capital (80 per cent from the United States) enters those areas its owners feel will return the greatest profits, not those having the greatest meaning for positive development; most of the benefits accrue to the investors. For example, from 1951 to 1963 new investments in Latin America from abroad totaled 6.9 billion dollars, while the return on these investments came to 11.9 billion—that is, a deficit of 5 billion dollars for Latin America. (It should be added that this refers only to net benefits; it does not take into account monies returning to investing nations because of license fees, grants, technical advice, and so forth.)[19]

In human terms this means—as Father Blase Bonpane wrote, on the basis of fifteen months work in Guatemala—that

over half the people are suffering from malnutrition. A wage of 50 cents a day in Guatemala is above average, but meat is 40 cents a pound and eggs 50 to 60 cents a dozen. This means that people don't eat and children die unnecessarily. Of the 70,000 a year who die in Guatemala, 30,000 are children. Guatemala's children mortality rate is forty times that of the United States.[20]

These conditions, plus the facts that socialism exists in much of the world including Latin America, and that the colonial system is clearly in decline, with masses everywhere in urgent motion, help to explain why significant religious leaders are speaking more and more frequently in terms of revolutionary traditions and needs. A striking paper was issued in July 1967 by fifteen bishops, seven of them from Latin America, called "Message to People of the Third World." It contains unequivocal language evoking the spirit of the prophets; thus, the message denounced "those forces of oppression that grind down the workers and the poor—feudalism, capitalism and imperialism."[21]

In the fall of 1967, three hundred priests in the leading cities of Brazil sent a letter to their Bishops in order "to communicate some of the serious concerns which afflict our consciences."[22] In a section of their letter headed "The Situation of the Brazilian People," they are described as "A Murdered People"; special note is taken of the fact that among the poor the infant morality rate often reaches 50 per cent. Such conditions, the priests insisted, "are ultimately problems of faith and religion." The priests noted charitable activities by the church but insisted that:

In practice, its line of action has been to coexist with this brutal exploitation, trying only to alleviate individual cases of sickness and misery. This has resulted in two negative factors: the need to seek contributions from the wealthy and to curry the favor of political and governmental organs; and the assumption of tasks which actually belong to the unions, the secular world and the government. The basic need is not only to face courageously the rules that govern capitalist production, but to help the church attain complete freedom from economic powers.

The priests condemned the ostentation of the church and added: "False notions of unworldliness have kept the church socially segregated from the masses, more at home with the middle classes, the bourgeoisie, then with the laborer, the impoverished peasant, the urban worker or the university student." These priests denounced the tactic of anticommunism used as a smear device and pledged themselves to live "the role of the prophet": to live simply among the masses, "to participate in the common life," and to help

142

end social and economic injustices.

At least one of the bishops so addressed needed no nudging; indeed, Bishop Jorge Marcos de Oliveira of Sante Andre declared early in 1968 that he "would accept a popular armed revolution" against conditions of hunger and oppression.[23] In Argentina, too, where the church is state-established (as it is in Bolivia, Paraguay, Peru, and Venezuela) and where the hierarchy remains notably conservative, "hundreds" of priests are affirming, according to a *New York Times* report, that if within fifteen years, "the church and the nation have not both undergone a deeply rooted social revolution, Argentina will become Marxist." "Many young churchmen," this report states, "feel that there are social currents afoot in Latin America that will not stop short of sweeping agrarian reform, nationalization of foreign industries and vastly increased benefits for the working class." A young priest, selected as representative of these "many," and who found it necessary to remain anonymous, said: "It all comes to this: Some kind of a revolution is coming. That much all of us know. We can get our hands muddy and maybe bloody, and help to lead that revolution. Or we can sit back in our comfortable parishes and wait until the revolution sweeps over us and drowns us. I've made my choice."[24]

Helping to explain the remarkably challenging stance taken in mid-1969 by the Peruvian government vis-à-vis the United States is the fact that in a plenary meeting in January Peru's bishops issued a statement holding "the imperialist international economic system and the Peruvian oligarchy responsible for social injustice" in their country. These injustices reflected particularly in grossly unfair land distribution, amounted to a "state of sin," said the bishops; "extremes of wealth and poverty" were endangering the nation and required elimination.[25] Bishop Juan F. Pepen y Soliman of the Dominican Republic also publicly denounced social and economic injustices rampant in his country. Insisting that "rural property in the Dominican Republic is so badly distributed that our recovery and economic development is impossible on the basis of the present system of landholding," the Bishop went on to warn that mass rebellions—as that in Vietnam—often arose because of such maldistribution. The one-crop system maintained in the Republic for purposes of enriching the few was "asphyxiating," he said, and the misuse of the Republic's land violated all concepts of justice as well as of "social economy." At a subsequent press conference, the President of the Republic referred to the Bishop's pastoral letter, adding that questions of property rights and legal use of governmental power made it impossible to undertake the suggested reforms. Bishop Pepen replied by citing documents from Vatican II affirming the priority of human rights over property rights and insisting that, where serious injury was done to the common good, the government had not only the right but the duty to act, and, if necessary, to expropriate and redistribute property.[26]

Even in Paraguay—also with a state-established church and perhaps the most reactionary and autocratic government in South America—"a serious challenge" to that government is coming from church figures, including some bishops, who "openly describe themselves as revolutionaries." One of those permitting himself to be named and directly quoted was the Most Reverend Aníbal Maricevich Fleitas, bishop of Concepción. The country, he said, was poor because it was exploited, but it was "rich in injustice." It is his duty to teach not only of the faith but also of life here—"civic matters, agriculture, nutrition," and so on. "We are," he continued, "peaceful revolutionaries. We are unalterably opposed to the violence of bloodshed, but we solidly favor moral violence. To hope for development just by letting things take their course is daydreaming." When asked about the strong criticism against the United States leveled by many priests, Bishop Maricevich said: "In many ways the United States has developed at our expense. The foreign policy of the United States is a policy without justice or charity. The great countries, including the United States, have developed themselves by sucking up the wealth of the small ones like Paraguay. Capitalism has no conscience."[27]

Such developments within religious circles, especially in the Roman Catholic church, while very dramatic within Latin America are by no means confined to that portion of the globe. Thus, for example, in March 1968 the Canon of the Malaga diocese in Spain, Father Gonzales Ruiz, urged all Christians to "commit themselves to the socialist revolution," since, he held, "true Christianity cannot prevail in a capitalist society."[28] In such a society, this priest said,

144

Christianity can only have a missionary role; believing, as he did, that "there is no alternative to capitalism other than socialism," and that the former represents the functioning of "a permanent unjust aggressor," the place of a Christian must be with the working people in their struggle to end such aggression and revolutionize society.

In the United States, also, the awareness that the crisis of the cities—which means, in our overwhelmingly urban civilization, a societal crisis—derives basically from the private ownership of land and buildings within the cities and the consequent private profit-making aim of such possession, which permeates the best of the secular analysis (as that by Charles Adams and Hans Blumenfeld), appears with increasing frequency in religious writings, notably in the works of the late Martin Luther King, Jr., and in such periodicals as *The Christian Century*.[29]

Data on the United States, while not disclosing the general impoverishment characteristic of Latin America, do demonstrate sufficient exploitation, poverty, and oppression to evoke revolutionary sentiments and activities from professionally religious people. To cite but one set of figures: in Detroit in 1967, the infant mortality rate per 1,000 live births in the most affluent section of the city was 12.1, but in the poorest section the rate was 69.1! Simultaneously, in 1968, the Government provided three billion dollars as a farm price subsidy, over 65 per cent of which went to agriculturists with incomes above $20,000 a year; for example, James O. Eastland of Sunflower County, Mississippi, supplements his salary as a U.S. Senator with $157,000 yearly from the Government for *not* producing cotton on his land.

It is the conditions producing such data that provoke an American priest, Father James Groppi of Milwaukee, to declare (explicitly making reference to Latin America):

We agree completely with the Bishop of Panama who said: "When we talk about the use of violence in the struggle for equality, we're not talking so much about morality as we are talking about tactics." So if you want to discuss violence as a tactic—that's another question. But I'll have nothing to do with a discussion of the morality of violence. I've read just a little too much, seen a little too much.

... Violence is many things. It's watching little black children go to bed at night wondering whether or not the rats will come through the wall and bite them. It's sitting in the house for two weeks with overcoats on and wrapped in blankets trying to keep warm. Violence is watching the kids across the street walk out of the house without any shoes on. It's knowing they're wondering whether they'll get a next meal. .... What are we supposed to do? Submit to this kind of system?[31]

It was in New York City, just after relief payments for about 900,000 people had been cut, that a Lutheran minister, Reverend James Gunther, speaking on behalf of the Interfaith Citywide Coordinating Committee Against Poverty, stated: "With the immoral decisions of the Legislature in regard to the health, education and welfare of the people, we believe that it may be, to bring about the changes needed, we will have to support the positive use of violence."[32]

The most striking illustration of the shifts in recent religious thinking on social questions, property, and revolution, bringing that thinking very much closer to that which dominated early Christianity, appears in certain encyclicals coming from the present Pope and his immediate predecessor. These reflect basic shifts in Vatican thinking on questions about the role of women, on equality of humankind, on the nature of property, on the question of war, and on the question of revolution. Dramatic alteration appears also in terms of the hitherto intensely hostile approach toward unbelievers and in particular toward Marxism, toward socialists, and, even, toward Communists. When one recalls that as recently as 1949 a decree of the Holy Office declared that all who actively supported Communist parties in any manner would be denied the sacrament, and compares this with pronouncements and practices of the Vatican during the 1960s, the dimensions of the shift become clear.[33]

Of central consequence is the change in the Vatican's approach toward private property. From Leo XIII on that approach had insisted—despite the contrary view of Thomas—that private property was a natural right and a right absolutely fundamental to civilized society, reflecting immutable "human nature." But, especially in *Populorum progressio* (March 1967), Pope Paul VI repudiates this view of private property. There one finds reflected in

146

particular the polemics of Emmanuel Mounier and of Cardinal Lercaro, archbishop of Bologna, against the concept of the right to private property as being an immutable and a natural one. They insisted that this stemmed not from biblical text but rather from Roman law. And the Pope quotes from none other than Ambrose, and from exactly that part of his writings hitherto signally neglected by the Church. For Ambrose is quoted to establish the idea that "the earth was given to all, not just the rich," and the Pope here specifically says that "private property is not an absolute and unconditional right for anybody," and that "wherever a conflict arises between acquired property rights and the cardinal needs of society, it is up to the public authority to resolve the conflict with the active participation of persons and groups."

Explicitly, even dramatically, the encyclical adds that "the public good invokes expropriation of some possessions if—by virtue of their size, partial or complete disuse and the consequent poverty of the population and damage to the interests of the country—they represent an obstacle to collective prosperity." It would not be easy to find language more descriptive of the unjust conditions of property ownership and distribution in large parts of the world—especially in those parts called "underdeveloped"—than these words of the Pope. Single-minded concentration upon the private appropriation of profit is denounced by Pope Paul, and the so-called "free exchange" reflective of so-called "free enterprise" is also held to have been found wanting in human benefit.

Further, the Pope said: "Revolutionary insurrection except in case of evident and prolonged tyranny that threatens gravely the fundamental rights of persons and dangerously injures the common good of the nation, will produce new injustices." But, as one South American priest immediately pointed out: "Both in and out of the continent many Christians and non-Christians will describe the situation of many Latin American nations precisely by using the terms covered by that 'exception.' "[34]

No wonder the distinguished savant, William L. Buckley, suggested in one of his ineffable columns that for some strange reason the Pope had put forth a "perfumed Marxism" and that the *Wall Street Journal* regretted the Pope's "confused Marxism." As a

147

Marxist, however, I must admit that the Pope's encyclical was enunciating, in a fairly mild, though significant form, the traditional levelism and the original revolutionary quality of Christianity; on both these matters, I will confess, Marxism is a latecomer.

Reference has been made to the widespread belief that we are in a post-Constantine if not a post-Christian era, or a postreligious one. At least as widespread in the United States is the idea that we are in a post-Marxist one. Affirming the obsolescence or, at least, irrelevance of Marxism is commonplace in this country. While noting the proliferation of God-is-dead literature, one must observe that a somewhat similarly entitled book reflects the Marxism-is-dead literature: *The God That Failed* (1960), edited by Richard Crossman, and with essays by distinguished figures who, having mistakenly believed in the divinity of Marx and/or Lenin and/or some particular Communist party, quite naturally found themselves disappointed, if not betrayed.

Similarly, while I have referred to the crisis in capitalist societies, an insistence upon the crisis in socialist societies is commonplace in the United States. Yet, I think the latter, to the degree that it does exist, reflects the newness of the venture and its unprecedented audacity, the forms and ferocity of the opposition it met and meets (not least from institutionalized religion), the areas in which it first appeared and developed, and inevitable difficulties of expansion and growth as well as problems of "success."

This is neither the place to develop an overall evaluation of the meaning of the socialist transformation, nor to argue at any length the relevance of Marxism for the United States. On the latter point, perhaps it will suffice to note that quite apart from the growing number of Americans who affirm that they are Marxists, one sees an insistence upon Marxism's consequence from such scholars as the late C. Wright Mills, and from Sidney Lens, William A. Williams, Staughton Lynd, Howard L. Parsons, George H. Hampsch, Robert S. Cohen, Dale Riepe, Richard Lichtman, Herbert Marcuse, and others. One observes also such a phenomenon as conferences on Marxism held regularly now, as at Notre Dame and at the University of Santa Clara, at meetings of the American Philosophical Association and of the American Sociological Association. Perhaps convincing certification of Marxism's relevance has appeared now that a recent *New York Times Book Review* feature admitted that it had been "all too easy to be patronizing or supercilious about the Marxian apparatus."[35] The *Book Review* even went on to admit the subtlety of "serious Marxian analysis"; perhaps some of us shall live to see the day when the *New York Times* actually permits such analysis in its pages.

The evidence suggests that the advocacy of Marxist-religious *rapprochment* need not be confined to the practical. That is, it is not uncommon now, both from the Marxist and the religious sides, to see cooperation advocated in terms of deeds or "works." This has been the emphasis—where the matter has been considered—on the Marxist side at least since the 1930s; from the religious side this emphasis was central to the whole Christian Socialist movements of the nineteenth and twentieth centuries in Europe and in the United States, where it was advocated with general consistency by such figures as Walter Rauschenbusch, Harry F. Ward, and A. J. Muste. It is at least implicit in the kind of historical analysis offered, for example, by Harvey Cox, and he has on occasion made it explicit; it is in almost explicit form in *Social Revolution and the New Latin America*, referred to earlier. In it, the Reverend Mark C. McGrath writes:

There is nothing good and holy in the Marxist premises which is not better set forth in that Christian attitude towards the world which the Second Vatican Council is now studying. . . . We, too, desire and work for an expansion of all material means of production and welfare, so that in our century, for the first time in recorded history, all men may [have] access to a material standard and an education which will free them from bodily want and the sad, almost animal dimness of life without knowledge, without culture, without joy, without beauty, without love.

Where Michael Novak calls for "The Revolution of 1976" that would see "a fundamental realignment of the bases of economic and political power in this land," he certainly speaks as a Christian, albeit one wedded to the leveling teachings and practices of early

149

Christianity; in doing this he is affirming not only a certain congruence in practice between Marxists and Christians, but also in theory.[36] That there is this theoretical affinity has not been emphasized in the literature, including the literature of "dialogue." Indeed, the contrary has been done by both sides. Such emphasis, where it excludes the other dimension, militates against fully implementing the practical cooperation widely suggested.

My argument is made almost verbatim from the opposite side by the late Martin Luther King, Jr., in the closing section of his final book:

> The Western nations that initiated so much of the revolutionary spirit of the modern world have now become the arch antirevolutionaries. This has driven many to feel that only Marxism has the revolutionary spirit. Communism is a judgment on our failure to follow through on the revolutions we have initiated. Our only hope today lies in our ability to recapture the revolutionary spirit and go into a sometimes hostile world declaring eternal opposition to poverty, racism and militarism.

If this cry is a judgment upon Christianity as practiced, it is a call in accordance with the deepest themes of Christianity; it is also a call in terms of the deepest currents in Marxism.

There is some doubt that the ethical theme is a component in Marxism; not infrequently, indeed, something approaching cynicism, if not worse, is attributed to the Marxist evocation of such a theme. For example, Julian N. Hartt of Yale's Divinity School recently wrote:

> Here the Christian revolutionary is up against an ally of the most formidable foremindedness, the dedicated Communist. The true believer of that sect freely—zealously indeed—uses value-charged terms but he is using them "scientifically." . . . Here we are struck by a curious flavor of theological consistency, since the Marxist does not believe that any spiritual power (good or evil) is causally efficacious in the movements of history.[37]

I appreciate Hartt's calling himself an "ally" even if his greeting is not quite fraternal, but when he says that the Marxist does not believe in the efficaciousness of good and evil in history he does not speak for me. The Marxists see the historical conditioning of all phenomena, including morality, but comprehending source and

150

origin is quite different from denying consequence and significance.

Any attempt to strip Marxism of its profoundly humanistic source and purpose is a caricature of Marxism. When Marx was 18 years old, writing *gymnasium* examination paper on "Reflections of a Youth on Choosing an Occupation," he began by insisting that man's "general good" was "to improve mankind and himself." He closed with two paragraphs that remain moving:

> History calls those the greatest men who ennobled themselves by working for the universal. Experience praises as the most happy the one who made the most people happy. Religion itself teaches us that the ideal for which we are all striving sacrificed itself for humanity, and who would dare destroy such a statement?

> When we have chosen the vocation in which we contribute most to humanity, burdens cannot bend us because they are only sacrifices for all. Then we experience no meager, limited, egotistic joy, but our happiness belongs to millions, our deeds live on quietly but eternally effective, and glowing tears of noble men fall on our ashes.[38]

This, of course, is the pre-Marxist Marx, but this dedication to ennoblement, this passion against injustice, this purpose to commence "the human epoch of history" is the heart of Marxism; divorcing that heart from the brain destroys Marxism.

If it has been possible to move from systems based on the private ownership of the means of production to socialism in one-third of the world, and the elimination therefrom of the private appropriation of profit, it may well be possible to move institutionalized religion from its present commitment to capitalism. That commitment ties such religion to a corpse, not to a living God; it certainly is not in accord with a reading of the original concepts and practices of such religions.

Evidence is not wanting that on both sides significant errors of interpretation and regrettable deeds were, and no doubt still are, committed. The nearly universal comdemnation of Marxism and of parties, movements, and revolutions dedicated to socialism issuing from religious institutions, and the active participation by such institutions in efforts aimed at thwarting such movements or overthrowing such revolutions, are matters of indisputable record. On the other hand, the expectation among some Marxists of the early demise of religion with the success of such revolutions and the violations of the Marxist principles denouncing anything smacking of religious persecution are also matters of indisputable record. While hostility persists on both counts and on both sides, it is not nearly as implacable and intense as it was; particularly as Prime Ministers of the USSR and popes of the Roman Catholic church repeatedly and passionately urge the necessity of peaceful coexistence. Given the presence of thermonuclear weapons, it is clear that old animosities are not only stale, they are positively anachronistic.

On neither side is the path of reason, comprehension, and cooperation a smooth one; notably in the United States, the strength of conservatism and of the Right is great. Nowhere is this more manifest than among the fundamentalists in religion; most conspicuous is the International Council of Christian Churches, founded in the United States in 1948 in direct and explicit opposition to the World Council of Churches. As of 1969, the ICCC conducted paid broadcasts via more than six hundred radio stations in the United States. Other groups of similar orientation and with influence are the Foundation for Christian Theology (Episcopal, based in Texas), and the Presbyterian Lay Committee (based in New York City).[39]

In 1957 a Gallup poll affirmed that 44 per cent of the people interviewed stated that churches should avoid any expression of views concerning social or political questions; in 1968, 53 per cent were of that opinion. That which is new, however, is the quality not of mutual hostility but of mutual curiosity and frequently respect. Of great importance here are the evidences of real and even heroic commitment to social progress and struggle on the part of religious figures, to which reference already has been made; on the other hand, non-Communist reports are multiplying to show an awareness on the part of religious sources of the altered attitude and practices by Marxist leaders and parties and states vis-à-vis religion. Examples of such reportage may be offered concerning the German Democratic Republic and Cuba. On the former, the articles by Markus Barth of the Pittsburgh Theological Seminary, after three months of study and inquiry, were quite remarkable. Hostility against the state and its socialist order were notable by their absence, Barth found; he thought, too, that under the new conditions a revival of the realities of Christianity were not only possible but were being witnessed. Of course, his report was by no means entirely positive, but its tone and content were hopeful and encouraging. He noted that while in the past, institutionalized religion in Germany had catered to the worst forms of repression and reaction, it now, in the socialist part of Germany, had the opportunity of functioning fully and with great freedom on behalf of positive social and economic developments. His experience suggested to him that: "Perhaps the best contribution we Western church members can make to our East German fellows is to abandon the equation 'Christianity is anticommunism' (or its alternative, 'all anticommunism supports true Christianity')."[40]

It is the opinion of Roland Warren, until recently the American Quaker representative in Germany, that: "Most Lutherans in both East and West Germany are convinced that the East German church is much healthier, much less materialistic, and more realistic in its approach to basic issues than the church in West German or in the United States."[41]

Ann Power, an English journalist, reported from Cuba for *Commonweal* (March 7, 1969) that the traditional tie of the church with reaction and colonialism resulted in persistent hostility among most of the priests (less so among the nuns) toward the Revolution and its present government; the government, on the other hand, she stated, went out of its way to assure the priests of its good will. The Apostolic Delegate maintains a friendly attitude toward the government and its social and economic efforts: "He is known and respected in government circles. He feels that the socialist revolution that Cuba is undergoing is necessary and good, and he feels the Latin American Church must play its part in the struggle for social justice, if the continent is to move out of terrible poverty and oppression without untold violence and bloodshed." We are told, in conclusion:

So there are three Churches in Cuba. The Church of the Revolution, of Camilo Torres and Fidel Castro (the Church as they wish it was); the Church of the growing generation, more open and committed than the pre-revolutionary Church; and the structured Church, the Church that survived the Revolution without changing its beliefs or its practices, the

Church of the priests and the Catholic Schools.

A Protestant view was offered by John A. Mackay, president emeritus of Princeton Theological Seminary and professor of Hispanic thought at American University in Washington. Mackay, who has visited Cuba since 1928, found in Castro's Cuba "no evidence of religious persecution"; the religious remained "opposed to Communism" but among them all,

adults and youth are one in feeling that Christianity in their homeland is confronted today with the greatest challenge and opportunity in its history. It is their reasoned conviction that the moment was never more opportune to confront fellow Cubans with the revolutionary significance of Jesus Christ, the gospel and the Church. Moreover, it is their judgment that in pursuing this objective they enjoy the necessary religious freedom.[42]

Finally, concerning the quite small Jewish population in Cuba, there is the very recent testimony of Everett Gendler, former rabbi at the Jewish Center in Princeton, New Jersey, who also served as rabbi in Mexico and Brazil, and who spent many months in 1968 and 1969 studying in Latin America, including Cuba. He found the five congregations that existed in 1958 still functioning; Jewish education, for those desiring it, is available; food requirements for the pious are met. Gendler chose to summarize the feelings he found in extensive quotations, all of which should be read in the original essay; the following two citations, however, should convey the spirit of the whole:

Rabbi, we say we believe all men are brothers, but we don't live that way. I win, you lose; I profit, you suffer. That's how we used to live here, and when the revolution first happened, I thought communism was something evil, a curse word. But slowly I've changed my mind, and I see that here at least it means we help one another, we gain or we lose together, we eat or we go hungry together. Is that bad, Rabbi? Is that evil? Isn't that what our religion teaches?

The Rabbi himself, while not closing his eyes to the persistence of problems and iniquities—"it is not utopia," as he writes—concludes that

154

nowhere in the Western Hemisphere have I seen a society in which there is such morale, such social dedication, such feelings of fellowship, such concern for children and young people. Nowhere have I seen in practice such a radical interpretation of human brotherhood expressed in the attempt at economic equality and sharing (not yet fully achieved) which converts from theory to fact the notion of our human interdependence.[43]

I think it would not be easy to find a more apt summary of the highest human values of the Judaeo-Christian tradition than that offered by this rabbi as being implemented today by the revolutionary government of Cuba.

Of the religions of the oppressed studied by Lanternari, he writes:

The messianic movements are movements of the people as well as movements of innovation. Within the religious dynamics of their society they highlight the critical "moment" at which tensions and differences have reached a climax—the moment between traditional forms too static to move ahead and the new challenge to religious life. Because these movements are both popular and revolutionary, new and able to renew, because they are spurred by the urgent and vital needs of oppressed people and societies caught in a dilemma, they look to the future and to the regeneration of the world.[44]

Christianity, too, had these origins and commitments; is it still able to renew?[45] Certainly, Marxism had fundamentally similar origins and basically identical commitments. Is it necessary that we —those of us who are religious and those of us who are Marxists —be the strange kind of allies Hartt pictured?

When the World Council of Churches said at its 1966 Geneva conference, "We recognize the need for fundamental changes in the structure of society," and added that the duty of Christianity today was "to speak a radical 'no' "; when, in the documents of Vatican II we read that while the Roman Catholic church in the eighteenth and nineteenth centuries cast itself "in the role of intransigent resistance to movements of social revolution," but that today "the Church intends to play its true historic role as a champion of human rights and to align itself with those who fight for those rights," and when the documents conclude that "neglecting temporal duties . . . jeopardizes eternal salvation"—when the two major bodies of world Christianity announce these views and make these promises, then this "dedicated Communist" (to use Hartt's language) is moved to say, with a joyous heart, Amen![46]

Chapter Eleven

Marxism, Religion, and the Future

Symbolic of the change in the realities of today's world—not least, of religion's approach to Marxism and Marxism's approach to religion—is the fact that the magnificent reliefs made for the Door of Death at St. Peter's in Rome and the bronze bust of Pope John XXIII, which today graces the Vatican Library, are the creation of the Communist artist, Giacomo Manzu.[1]

And none will deny that Dublin has been a bastion of Catholic conservatism; yet in 1968 the General Secretary of the Irish Workers' [Communist] party and a Jesuit priest, Father Michael Sweetman, marched through the streets of Dublin arm-in-arm in a demonstration protesting the eviction of slum dwellers. When questioned about this on television, Father Sweetman said that bad housing meant bad family conditions, and the family, according to the church's teachings, was society's basic unit; Michael O'Riordan, veteran of the Spanish Civil War, frequent political prisoner, and a Communist leader, said for his part that, "The first Christian was regarded as an agitator." Whatever may have been true in the past, in the present this Irish priest and this Irish Communist leader found themselves together in a common effort on behalf of the despised and the forsaken. Despite the probable surprise and the possible suspicion, surely regard, maybe even love, grew on both sides.[2]

Still, let none be oversanguine. John Kenneth Galbraith, turning to the novel form, has one of his most sympathetic characters say: "Some American officials, we must face it, are not easy to reassure. If you are not a Communist, they suspect you of being a stooge. If you are too smart to be a stooge, they suspect you of being a stalking horse. If assured on all these counts, they still conclude you are an opening to the Left."[3] With enough stalking horses, stooges, and Communists, the opening to the Left may yet become as serious in the United States as it already has become in Catholicism's heartland.

Marxism's strategic commitment, I repeat, is to the ennoblement of man. It is not to the working class; it is not to revolution; it is not to socialism. It believes that in this era, its commitment to man's ennoblement requires a basic transformation in the structure and superstructure of those societies characterized by the private possession of the means of production and the conducting of production and distribution fundamentally for purposes of private aggrandizement, that is, it requires a revolution.[4] It believes that the central force for this kind of revolution is that class divested of the means of control but placed at the center of production, namely, the working class, and that the name of the social order born of such transformation—varied as it will be and has been in form—will be socialism.

All these are beliefs based on considerable thought and analysis as well as, by now, not inconsiderable experience; it cannot be emphasized too often that Marxism's commitment is to man's ennoblement. If that is forgotten, one may get fanaticism, but not Marxism. The Marxist vision is not of perfection; it is of improvement and of progress, but to this no termination is projected, and given the dynamic essence of Marxism such projection would be contradictory. It is worth emphasizing this latter point for the contrary is often charged to Marxism; its alleged envisioning of an "end" to history, of the achievement of perfection and universal happiness, is held to be among its signal errors—especially the characteristic differentiating it from religion, and from Christianity in particular.

Harvey Cox, for example, believes that Marxism's future orientation is "spoiled" by the "mistaken belief that after one more surge, history would be finished and man would triumph once and for all." He continues: "Marx saw in the classless society an end to the motion generated by class conflict."[5] Marx saw that end, but this did not mean to him, nor does it mean to Marxism, that "history would be finished." It does mean that past history's basic dynamic, class struggle, would no longer function, but this does not mean that other dynamics—the contest with nature, the development of science in general, and the process of criticism and self-criticism, for example—would no longer exist.

The French Jesuit theologian, Henri de Lubac, writing on "The New Man: The Marxist and the Christian View," finds that both Marxism and Christianity project the achievement of perfection and completion, but that the latter sees this as God's work and related to the coming of the Kingdom of Heaven. Then, with "the achievement of the Mystical Body of Christ," there will be an end to tensions and antagonisms with perfect unity fully realized. But Marxism, according to de Lubac, sees this not as resulting from supernatural intervention but rather "as the natural end of an immanent process." And this, he exclaims, "without any new principle being introduced into this humanity"; he is persuaded that it is Marxism and not Christianity that, in this, expects the greater miracle.[6]

In reply: First, there is a new principle introduced into humanity, and that principle results from the termination of class struggle. Marxism thinks that with the human stage of history a new humanity will have already begun, else that stage could not be reached and the new stage—socialism— appear. It will make possible the further nurturing of a new humanity, one capable of achieving communism and then, in communism, further growing.

Secondly, Marxism does not affirm the end of contradiction with the achievement of socialism, or even of communism. It does project the termination of antagonistic contradiction, that is, contradiction containing within it antagonism of a basic and organic quality that constantly war with each other and that, for resolution, require the extinction of one by the other, with the other then transformed. But the problems of advancing science remain; the challenge of nature persists; the errors and failings of people recur; differences of views and emphases among people persist; and intensely critical examination and reexamination of failings and difference and projects will continue, indeed, will be encouraged.

Further, Marxism, unlike Utopian Socialism (as formulated by Owen and Fourier), never asserted that with rational social reorganization all human problems would thereby be resolved. Personal and family problems, tragedies, catastrophes, and dilemmas no doubt will continue, though it is hoped that with the development of the psychological and biological sciences and the elevation of social amenities and facilities many of these problems will be eased. In this sense, also, perfection is not projected by Marxism, and the achievement of the social order it envisions will not assure universal happiness. It will greatly alleviate suffering and will make possible the fuller development of human capacities; fortunately, however, the inhabitants of a future communist world will not be without their problems and their challenges.

It is relevant to add—particularly since it seems to have rarely been noticed—that Marx commented upon the significance to historical development, at various stages, of nature itself and of man's effort to master it. For example, in *Capital*, he refers to the fact that "apart from the degree of development, greater or less, in the form of social production, the productiveness of labor is fettered by physical conditions." Among these he selected two for emphasis: the constitution of man himself and "surrounding Nature." Concerning the latter, he continues:

The external physical conditions fall into two great economic classes, 1) Natural wealth in means of subsistence, *i.e.*, a fruitful soil, waters teeming with fish, etc., and 2), natural wealth in the instruments of labor, such as waterfalls, navigable rivers, wood, metal, coal, etc. At the dawn of civilization, it is the first class that turns the scale; at a higher stage of development, it is the second.[7]

Science is the postulate of Marxism. It is sometimes forgotten that the victory of science over nature was achieved only in the past two or three centuries. As A. R. Hall of Cambridge University has written: "Magic and esoteric mystery—the elements of the irrational—were not firmly dissociated from serious science before the seventeenth century. ..." He adds: "Rational science, then, by whose methods alone the phenomena of nature may be rightly understood, and by whose application alone they may be controlled, is the creation of the seventeenth and eighteenth centuries."[8]

The insistence here that only through science may natural phenomena be comprehended, and only with the same principles may they be controlled—the crowning achievements of the ages of Enlightenment and Reason—form the foundation of Marxism. Marxism, however, insists that that which is true for nature is true also for man. That is, Marxism holds that science not only can explicate nature and produce effective controls over it (and that nothing else can), but that science may also explicate society and produce effective controls for it, thus enhancing man's power not only over his natural environment but over his social environment as well. As the one infinitely enhances man's condition and potential, so the other will improve both; the two together—mastery over nature and over society—can bring man out of the Kingdom of Necessity into the Kingdom of Freedom.

The triumph of the principles of science in the area of nature was a most difficult and prolonged process. Its difficulty lay not only in the direct intellectual challenge involved, but also in the fact that there were enormous vested interests and powerful institutions and deep superstitions that found themselves challenged by those principles and therefore offered stubborn resistance to their victory. All these considerations—the profound intellectual difficulties and the extraneous hazards and obstacles—are present where the victory of science in society is concerned. They are, in fact, intensified; the intellectual difficulties because the problems are more elusive, more subtle, and more permeated by subjectivity; the extraneous hazards and obstacles because the challenge of science in society is more frontal, more devastating, more total to vested interests, powerful institutions, and deep superstitions than in the case of science's challenge to nature.

Only when technique has reached the point where the age-old burdens of humanity—impoverishment, illiteracy, inequality, war —can be successfully and totally overcome, and only when the class appears whose objective interests are opposed to the maintenance of injustice and oppression so fundamentally that its victory will make possible not only its own liberation but also, and therefore, man's liberation—only when these two related phenomena appear is it possible to achieve a science of society. The working class, having no real interest in injustice, has no real interest in deception; hence, only now in our era, when the replacement of capitalism by socialism is characteristic, are we witnessing the triumph of science in society.

The victory of science in nature, to the degree that it has been accomplished, took many centuries and was accompanied by awful tragedies, errors, and crimes. Nor with its triumph has its form and content been fixed; on the contrary, as the detection of error is a precondition for science's advance, so the incompleteness of its grasp of reality is both a part of its nature and a guarantee of its continual development. There is, perhaps, some reason to hope that with the accelerated pace of historical development, the triumph of science in society may take fewer centuries. There is no reason to believe that the victory here, where the contest is more difficult, can be achieved without tragedy, error, and crime. On the contrary, alas, the relatively brief history of this contest already affords abundant evidence of all three.

A fundamental conflict exists between the development and application of science in society and the nature and idea of capitalism. Robert Heilbroner has developed this point perceptively. "The world of science as it is applied to society is committed to the idea of man as a being who shapes his collective destiny," he writes; "the world of capitalism to an idea of man as one who permits his common social destination to take care of itself." He goes on:

The essential idea of a society built on scientific engineering is to impose human will on the social universe; that of capitalism to allow the social universe to unfold as if it were beyond human interference.

Before the activist philosophy of science as a social instrument, this inherent social passivity of capitalism becomes archaic, and eventually intolerable. The "self-regulating" economy that is its highest social achievement stands condemned by its absence of meaning and intelligence, and each small step taken to correct its deficiencies only advertises the inhibitions placed on the potential exercise of purposeful thought and action by its remaining barriers of ideology and privilege. In the end, capitalism is weighed in the scale of science and found wanting, not alone as a system but as a philosophy.[9]

Heilbroner warns that while "Science is a majestic driving force from which to draw social energy and inspiration," "its very impersonality, its 'value-free' criteria, may make its tutelary elites as remote and unconcerned as the principles in whose name they govern." This certainly is possible if science is held to be "value-free"; but such an attitude negates science. Since the commitment of science is to truth and since its methodology revolves around and exists in order to ascertain truth, nothing could be less "value-free" than science. To ascertain reality is the first and indispensable step toward comprehension and therefore toward effective action; where this is forgotten one may get clerks or monsters but he will not have scientists. For these reasons, as well as those submitted by Heilbroner, capitalism is deeply antiscientific (related to the thought of Keynes, already cited, that it is "irreligious"); for these reasons, Marxism rejects capitalism and embraces science.

As applied to society, science has the same fluid, process-filled character as when it treats of nature; here as everywhere and always the chief enemy of science is dogma. Marxism is a system of thought, not of memory. To be able to remember is indispensable, but only as an element in the process of thinking. It may not be out of place—though there be a touch of irony in it—to bring authority to bear on this question of dogma versus science. Earlier I quoted Engels briefly to this effect; I also offered a brief extract from some relevant remarks by Lenin. Now it is useful to quote Lenin at greater length, here from "Our Program" (1899):

There can be no strong socialist party without a revolutionary theory which unites all socialists, from which they draw their convictions, and which they apply in their methods of struggle and means of action. To defend such a theory, which to the best of your knowledge you consider to be true, against unfounded attacks and attempts to corrupt it is not to imply that you are an enemy of *all* criticism. We do not regard Marx's theory as something completed and inviolable; on the contrary, we are convinced that it has only laid the foundation stone of the science which socialists *must* develop if they wish to keep pace with life. We think then an *independent* elaboration of Marx's theory is especially essential for Russian socialists; for this theory provides only general *guiding* principles, which, *in particular,* are applied in England differently than in France, in France differently than in Germany, and in Germany differently than in Russia.[Lenin's italics.][10]

Marxism, being scientific, is revolutionary. Its essential purpose is the elimination of exploitation and oppression; today this means, I think, the elimination of monopoly capitalism, colonialism, racism, impoverishment, and war. In Marx's words, "all relations, all conditions, in which man is a humiliated, enslaved, despised creature, must be destroyed." Were there no such conditions there would be no revolutionary philosophy, no revolutionary movement, and no Marxism. Said Marx, in commenting on the ideas and organizations of socialism just after the Paris Commune had been drowned in blood in 1871: "The soil out of which it grows is modern society itself. It cannot be stamped out by any amount of carnage. To stamp it out the Government would have to stamp out the despotism of capital over labor—the conditions of their own parasitical existence." One may profitably contrast this analysis and prophecy with the somewhat premature exclamation of Thiers, who had presided at the extermination of the Communards: "Now we have finished with Communism!"

Since over twenty per cent of the French electorate votes Communist, it would be difficult for some French wit to maintain its irrelevance; in the United States, however, insistence upon Marxism's irrelevance or obsolescence has been a repeated refrain. In the McCarthy era, when neoconservatism was dominant, this refrain reached deafening proportions. Today, however, what with Vietnam and Cuba ninety miles away and Marxist-inspired militancy manifest among millions of youth, blacks, and impoverished people, the volume is muted. Now that even Presidents belatedly notice the existence of poverty and racism and Senators discover America to be "a sick society," it would be quite superfluous to bring forward, yet again, the evidence of decay, disintegration, and delerium all about us.

Two items are of interest here. In 1968 Senator James O. Eastland of Mississippi was paid a subsidy of over $13,000 each month by the U.S. Government for not growing cotton on his plantations in Sunflower County; a hungry child in Mississippi in 1968 received a total of $9 a month in welfare. Mike Gorman, executive director of the National Committee Against Mental Illness, in preparing a report for the Government in 1969, stated that there were four million emotionally disturbed children in the country, and that about one million "are so ill they require immediate treatment." But care is available for only one-third of these; the rest "are bounced around from training schools to reformatories to jails." During the past decade, said Gorman, admission of teen-agers to state hospitals for the mentally ill had risen 150 per cent and most of the youths were "the worse for the experience."[11] If such data, in a land as rich as the United States, do not represent a situation crying out for revolution, then the crucifixion of Jesus was quite in vain.

The fact is that the historic scourges of man prevail widely in our country; the United States is riven with illiteracy, poverty, racism, and the preparing for and the waging of war. In the face of all this, to speak of the irrelevancy of Marxism, or of its alien and conspiratorial character, is a hallmark of ignorance and/or complicity in an effort to retain such abominations.

The reports of the United Nations demonstrate that a majority of mankind are chronically hungry, quite illiterate, live under conditions of indignity and inequality, and bear upon their shoulders the fearful burdens of paying for past wars, waging present ones, and preparing for new ones. Today productive developments and social organizations have reached the point where none of these need be endured any longer. Knowledge of this momentous fact is out now; the people of the world know that they can end their suffering and that the means exist for making a life of fruitfulness,

165

creativity, fraternity, and peace. It is this knowledge—not thermonuclear energy—that is the greatest force in the world today.

If one evaluates the accomplishments of revolutionary societies since 1917—weighing everything—it is difficult to see how one can conclude otherwise than that conditions of the bulk of the population in the postrevolutionary societies are markedly better than was true in the prerevolutionary societies.

A modest assessment comes from Robin Marris of Cambridge University:

Strictly socialist systems are slower to create consumer wants, but better adapted to meet, for example, the needs of the old and the poor, and in practice really do perform better in these areas. We have to admit that it is almost exclusively in the "free world" that we observe the extremes of poverty and affluence side by side.[12]

These extremes are certainly about us in the United States, and when they become too public, as in Resurrection City, they are bulldozed away. In Guayaquil, Ecuador, also part of the "free world," Paul Montgomery reports: "Probably the largest single 'industry' is on 18th Street, the red-light district. There, in a scene of unsurpassed wretchedness, perhaps four hundred girls stand outside their stalls on an average night. Some are little more than frightened children. The standard fee is 35 cents."[13] Three days later Montgomery reported from Macara, some two hundred miles south of Guayaquil, that hunger was rampant. He spoke with a physician who told him: "Already you begin to see the medical consequences of hunger. The people are weak, listless. The children's bones are brittle." The reporter asked, mimicking the state officials: "And what of communism and revolution?" The physician replied: "Those people [the officials] say everything is communism and revolution. But I tell you, friend, here everything is hunger. And hunger, friend, is a very heavy thing."

Father Blase Bonpane, a priest of the Maryknoll Order recently withdrawn from his mission in Guatemala, reported his conversation with a leader of the right wing there. The priest was told that the murder of the director of a youth center was being planned, because "I know he is a Communist and so we are going to kill

166

him." The priest asked: "How do you know?" And the report went on: " 'I know he is a Communist because I heard him say he would give his life for the poor.' With such a definition of Communist, we find many new names in the Communist ranks, including Christ's."[14]

Dr. Juan Bosch, former President of the Dominican Republic, now residing in Spain, asked in *The Christian Century*: "What is the blind force that keeps the United States from accepting the changes that have occurred in so many parts of the world, and that must inevitably extend to Asia and Latin America?" His answer: "The force is the same as that which leads the United States to wage war in Vietnam. On the surface, it is anti-communism, but that is merely the negative aspect of the real force: the profit motive. It is eagerness for profit that has made the United States the champion of the status quo everywhere in the world."[15]

Private profit and all that it connotes is fundamental; chauvinism and racism are related to it. James Colaianni recently summarized accurately, I believe, the conventional attitude of the Roman Catholic church—and not only of that church—a generation ago: "God had chosen to live in a white, capitalist, Western culture! Other cultures were either suspect or labeled outright diabolical."[16] Colaianni subtitled his work *The Crisis of Radicalism Within the Church*; few recent events illustrate this crisis more sharply than the furor that arose in the spring of 1968 when it was learned that among those receiving Christmas gifts in 1967 from His Holiness was Luigi Longo, general secretary of the Communist party of Italy. When the news broke—finally—an official spokesman for the Pontiff said that Paul's "paternal charity apparently has no bounds."[17]

In the election a few weeks later, eight and a half million Italians voted for the Party headed by Longo; this might well suggest to the official spokesman that apologies for charity dispensed to such a man were not needed. But then one reads the front-page editorial in the Rome newspaper, *Il Tempo*, voice of a section of the Curia: "A Saint, St. Louis of France, kissed the leper ... but the leper is not the devil. ... He who kisses the devil, who sends greetings to the devil, even with the most holy intentions, finds fire in his house." If it turns out that this is the kind of house the Vatican is to be in the future, one can only say it had better be very careful of "the fire next time."

Quite another Catholic tradition is that represented by Peter Maurin, who writes in the first issue of *The Catholic Worker* in May 1933:

> To blow the dynamite of a message is the only way to make a message dynamite. If the Catholic Church is not today the dominant social and dynamic force, it is because Catholic scholars have failed to blow the dynamite of the Church. It is about time to blow the lid off so the Catholic Church may again become the dominant dynamic social force.

That is a fine competition; let us see whose view—and activity—will be the dominant social dynamic force for the present and for the future!

There are strands in the religious history and thought of the United States—as in its sociopolitical history and thought—that offer special difficulties as well as special opportunities for the Marxist-Christian dialogue. The fundamentalist aspect with neo-conservative offshoots make up the great difficulties; these, permeated with racism (as one would expect for the United States) conceive of efforts for significant social change, let alone Marxism, as seditious and diabolical. On the other hand, the United States is the heart of the New World, the land of experimentation, of democracy, of equality, of republicanism, of deism, of pluralism, of Utopianism, of great militancy, of the first successful colonial revolution, of a decisive Civil War, "testing whether this nation or any nation so conceived" might long endure, in which half a million lives were lost and as a result of which chattel slavery was abolished and property to the tune of several billions of dollars was confiscated. Certainly here in the United States the great confrontation in religion between priest and prophet has occurred—and continues. And here in the United States the great confrontation between radical and conservative—between Jefferson and Hamilton, John Brown and Jefferson Davis, Calvin Coolidge and Eugene Debs, James Eastland and Henry Winston—has occurred and continues.

It is marvelously appropriate that the "discoverer" of this land, Columbus, remarked: "Gold constitutes treasure, and he who possesses it has all he needs in this world, as also the means of rescuing souls from Purgatory, and restoring them to the enjoyment of Paradise."[18] From that to the Reverend Russell Conwell, founder of Temple University, and his "Acres of Diamonds" oration, to John D. Rockefeller (original model) and his gilded temples and slaughtered miners is one strand.

The other is enunciated by Benjamin Franklin in his *Autobiography*, when he said: "That the most acceptable service of God was the doing of good to men." Theodore Roosevelt—in many respects a typical American—also possessed a religion which, to quote Morris R. Cohen, "to him means good deeds."[19] How one tries to "do good" is viewed differently by different people, of course, but that this is the basic test of godliness lies deep in the mainstream of religion in the United States. How far he went and that he went that far were particular features of John Brown, but that he viewed religion as acting on earth for men and women and especially for the least among them were features in the life of the man from Torrington, Connecticut, that remain central to religion in the United States.

In his great speech to the court prior to being sentenced John Brown stressed this view; it was a view that shook the nation because it reflected a central nerve in that nation. "This Court acknowledges, as I suppose, the validity of the Law of God," the martyr said.

I see a book kissed here which I suppose to be the Bible, or, at least, the New Testament. That teaches me that all things "whatsoever I would that men should do unto me I should do even so to them." I endeavored to act up to that instruction. I say, I am yet too young to understand that God is any respecter of persons. I believe that to have interfered as I have done, as I have always freely admitted I have done, in behalf of His despised poor, was not wrong, but right.

Virginia clergymen visited Brown in his cell. We are told:

"One of these gentlemen . . . said that he had called on Brown to pray with him. He said that Brown asked if he was ready to fight, if necessity required it, for the freedom of the slave. On his answering in the negative, Brown said that he would thank him to retire from his cell; that his prayers would be an abomination to his God. To another clergyman he said that he would not insult his God by bowing down with any one who had the blood of the slave upon his skirts.[20]

In kind, this was Emerson's religion, too. In *English Traits* (1856), for example, we find Emerson writing:

The church at this moment is much to be pitied. She has nothing left but possession. If a Bishop meets an intelligent gentleman, and reads fatal interrogations in his eyes, he has no resource but to take wine with him. False position introduces cant, perjury, simony, and even a lower class of mind and character, into the clergy; and when the hierarchy is afraid of theology, there is nothing left but to quit a church which is no longer one.

These concepts and criticisms helped to induce the particular American phenomenon of Unitarianism. Its main distinguishing feature did not really revolve upon questions of the Trinity, but upon the Unitarian's insistence that the central point of religion was its concern with man. Earlier I quoted the key passages from the seminal writings of William Ellery Channing demonstrating this central concern with humankind and its activity on earth.

Following in a direct line from this kind of religion was the immensely influential Walter Rauschenbusch, for many years professor of church history at the Rochester Theological Seminary. Probably his single most widely read book, *Christianity and the Social Crisis* (which remains in print), has left a lasting impression upon American intellectual and religious life. Rauschenbusch speaks freely of his conviction that the logic of Jesus led to socialism. Thus:

Socialism is the ultimate and logical outcome of the labor movement. When the entire working class throughout the industrial nations is viewed in a large way, the progress of socialism gives an impression of resistless and elemental power . . . independence and equality for the working class must mean the collective ownership of the means of production and the abolition of the present two-class arrangement of industrial society.

"It is inevitable," he went on, "that those who stand against conditions in which most men believe and by which the strongest profit, shall suffer for their stand." But, "The championship of social justice is almost the only way left open to a Christian nowadays to gain the crown of martyrdom. Theological heretics are rarely persecuted now. The only rival of God is mammon, and it is only when his sacred name is blasphemed that men throw the Christians to the lions." Religion's duty, Rauschenbusch concluded, was to "turn the present unparalleled economic and intellectual resources of humanity to the harmonious development of a true social life."[21] This is the religion of Kirby Page, Sherwood Eddy, A. J. Muste, Stephen Wise, Dorothy Day, Martin Luther King, Jr., Harry Ward, Willard Uphaus, William Howard Melish, and Claude Williams.[22]

James Forman's demand for reparations from dominant white America is widely held to be "shocking" and "absurd"; that he so far has concentrated upon the churches of America is supposed to intensify the uncouthness; actually, it represents a mark of respect since it demonstrates the hope that from that institution above all others positive response might be forthcoming.

While institutional religion in the United States has a very bad record concerning slavery and racism—and so owes reparations really beyond mere money—the prophetic quality in religion as practiced often by Americans certainly formed an essential feature of abolitionism as a whole. Perhaps if that movement and its deep radicalism were better understood (and taught), white America today would be less startled by the present black liberation effort. For example, though everybody knows *Uncle Tom's Cabin*, one wonders at times whether anybody still reads it. There one will find Forman's arguments almost in full, and he will find his language, word for word. Thus we read:

> Does not every American Christian owe to the African race some effort at reparation for the wrongs that the American nation has brought upon them? Shall the doors of churches and school-houses be shut upon them? ... If it must be so, it will be a mournful spectacle. If it must be so, the country will have reason to tremble, when it remembers that the fate of nations is in the hands of One who is very pitiful and of tender compassion.

She warned: "A mighty influence is abroad, surging and heaving the world, as with an earthquake. And is America safe? Every nation that carries in its bosom great and unredressed injustice has in it the elements of this last convulsion." Further (and the italics are Mrs. Stowe's):

> Both North and South have been guilty before God; and the *Christian Church* has a heavy account to answer. Not by combining together to protect injustice and cruelty, and making a common capital of sin, is this Union to be saved,—but by repentance, justice, and mercy; for, not surer is the eternal law by which the mill-stone sinks in the ocean, than that stronger law by which injustice and cruelty shall bring on nations the wrath of God![23]

Coming right out of Mrs. Stowe is the December 1967 address of Richard Shaull of Princeton Theological Seminary, "A Theological Perspective on Human Liberation":

> When the old order is no longer able to serve man adequately and is too sclerotic to change fast enough to keep up with events, it will have to be brought down or broken open by conflict and violence of one sort or another. And the dynamic of God's action in the world moves in that direction. The violence of the struggle will be determined primarily by those in power.[24]

A Marxist finds himself in full agreement with this, and would require the change of only one word—he would replace "God's" with the word, "mass"—and rest in agreement. Surely this holds high promise for a meaningful common dialogue.

From those who are deeply religious one finds a new and most urgent note of remarkably frank criticism of the religious Establishment. Thus in an editorial, *Commonweal* put the matter not only frankly but almost brutally:

> The Church has become increasingly irrelevant in our society, and increasingly restricted to the private sphere. Even the language of the institutional Church is that of another era, and the pomps it displays to the world are those of a feudal past. . . . The questions churchmen raise are meaningless to the young, and they are, in addition, scandalized and repelled by much of what they see in the institutional Church. . . . Nietzsche was wrong and God is not dead; it is the smell of decaying idols that bothers many people.[25]

Perhaps the most persuasive voice rising from the many who are within one or another church and who are calling for "Resistance in the Church" is the former Jesuit priest, Eugene C. Bianchi, now a professor at Emory University. He sees the content and essence of Christianity as a source of hope for the struggle that must be waged, he thinks, within the church to purify and to transform it. He concludes his essay:

The great human and material resources of the Church must not be wasted or abused. If we resist oppressive elements of the Church's past, it is for the sake of freeing it for renewed life and service today and tomorrow. The older model, however, will not be dismantled without considerable pain, struggle and misunderstanding. It is precisely at this point that we locate the value of creative resistance.[26]

Rather similarly on the Marxist side, it is now past its first century and in living form is no longer the isolated, beleaguered, and bleeding corpus of thirty or forty years ago. Its multinational reality inevitably induces challenges and changes; the unprecedented technical, scientific, demographic, and political developments of the past two decades similarly compel rethinking and new thinking. Marxism would not be Marxism if all this were not true; it is part of the essence of Marxism's beauty and validity that dynamism is of its very character. The problems are momentous, and efforts at solution would be difficult in any case; given the hostile forces that remain, given the manifest dangers that persist, and given normal institutional restraints, such efforts must be prodigious in the future if they are to succeed. But the efforts must be forthcoming since failure is unthinkable. Reflections of growth and change are clear everywhere in the universe of Marxism, and not least in thinking about and actions toward religion. From that side, this has also assisted and must continue to assist the dialogue that is mutually beneficial.

One finds now, for example, a leading Latin American Marxist writer, Roque Dalton of El Salvador, rejoicing that Marxist thought "has essentially overcome the 'infantile disorder' of abolishing religion right away, a view prevalent in our ranks for some time." He continues by remarking that Marxism and Christianity do not differ so much in terms of their ideals as they do in terms of their concepts of the origins of these ideals. He emphasizes, in any case, not differences, but rather "what unites Communists and Left Catholics," which, "above all, are their lofty dedication to the ideal, their desire for truth and justice, their constant search for spiritual values and their common stand against the dehumanization and fetishism imposed by modern capitalism." He rejects "the criteria of a decrepit anti-clericalism," comments on "real points of coincidence in the ideological sphere," and calls attention to the fact that Santiago Carillo, general secretary of the Communist party of Spain, has insisted that "there are spheres in the Marxist-Leninist ideology where not only coexistence but also coincidence, are possible, and this makes feasible cooperation in practice."[27]

Several years ago, Gus Hall, general secretary of the Communist party of the United States, in commencing his very positive evaluation of the encyclical *Pacem in Terris*, remarked self-critically:

> There are several concepts in the Party and its leadership that we could use this occasion to burn out, concepts that are a hindrance to our Party and especially to our united front relations. We must discard all concepts of cynicism, disdain and scoffing in our approach and deal with this Encyclical in the manner in which most Americans are already dealing with it, that is, with the utmost respect and seriousness.[28]

Hall insisted that it was necessary to "discard hangovers of syndicalist, anarchist and old Ingersoll attitudes which are deeply imbedded in our Party and its leadership."

The mutual process of reexamination comes out of the mutual necessity for common action against common foes: colonialism, hunger, poverty, illiteracy, all forms of inequality, all conditions demeaning to dignity, and imperialist war. This mutuality is the firmest guarantee that the processes of reasoning and acting together will persist and grow, whatever obstacles may be placed before those engaged in that process.

C. Wright Mills, in the book that appeared at the moment of his death, concluded: "Both Marxism and Liberalism embody the ideals of Greece and Rome and Jerusalem; the humanism of the renaissance, the rationalism of the eighteenth century enlightenment." He added: "Karl Marx remains the thinker who has articulated most clearly—and most perilously—the basic ideals which liberalism shares."[29] In seeing this continuity Mills wrote truly; in an opposite way Goebbels expressed the same thought when, entering Paris with the victorious Nazi troops, he exulted (somewhat prematurely): "Now we will finish with 1789 and 1917!"

In its dedication to the struggle against social evils still afflicting the majority of the human race, Marxism knows and emphasizes that its goals are common to those held by the partisans of the Enlightenment and upholders of all the great religions. Were Marxists alone in this dedication they would fail. They are not alone, however, and all who stand together, opposed to systematized exploitation and systematic extermination, will—exactly because of unity—overcome the forces of evil and fulfill the promise of man.

Notes

Chapter 1. Views and Problems: An Introduction

1. A very convenient compilation is: Karl Marx and Friedrich Engels, *On Religion* (Moscow: Foreign Languages Publishing House, 1957). Quotations in this chapter from both men are taken from this volume, which clearly identifies each source.

2. Note that Marx says "of the people," not "for the people."

3. There exists, of course, the opposite feeling, that is, the feeling on the part of religious people that the denial or absence of religion reflects moral idiocy, if not satanic possession. Even so sensitive a person as Charles C. West of the Princeton Theological Seminary will permit himself to write of "the way in which the Communist mind is warped" (*Communism and the Theologians* [New York: Macmillan Co., 1963], p. 45). One is reminded that Parson Adams, in Fielding's *Joseph Andrews*—and I apologize beforehand to Presbyterians—said: "The first care I always take is of a boy's morals; I had rather he should be a blockhead than an atheist or a Presbyterian."

4. J. H. Maurer, "Has the Church Betrayed Labor?," in *Labor Speaks for Itself on Religion*, ed. Jerome Davis (New York: Macmillan Co., 1929), pp. 30–31.

5. Walter M. Abbott, S.J., ed., *The Documents of Vatican II* (New York: Guild Press, 1966), pp. 241, 285.

6. Marx and Engels, *op. cit.*, p. 83.

7. Bohdan R. Bociurkiw, in *Lenin: The Man, the Theorist, the Leader*, eds. L. Shapiro, P. Reddaway, and P. Rosat (New York: Praeger, 1967), pp. 109-10.

8. *Ibid.*, p. 111.

9. *Ibid.*, p. 113.

10. See, for example, A. Deborin's foreword to the English edition of *Materialism and Empirio-Criticism*, written by Lenin in 1908, and published as volume 13 of

NOTES

Lenin's *Collected Works* (New York: International Publishers, 1927).

11. Joseph Needham, "Science, Religion and Socialism," in *Christianity and the Social Revolution,* eds. J. Lewis, K. Polanyi, and D. Kitchin (London: Gollancz, 1935), p. 438.

12. *Church News,* no. 8 (25 Feb. 1917); quoted by Julius F. Hecker in *Christianity and the Social Revolution, op. cit.,* pp. 306–7.

13. Lenin, *On Religion* (Moscow: Progress Publishers, 1965), quotations under specific essays named.

14. In France, the Workers' party, at its Twentieth National Congress in 1902, adopted this resolution:

> In the anti-clericalism which our rulers have been ostentatiously professing for some time past and which is only aimed at a certain number of orders in rebellion against their laws, the French Workers' Party can only see a new maneuver of the capitalist class to divert the workers from their struggle against economic slavery, the progenitor of all other forms of political and religious slavery.

In Maurice Thorez, *Catholics and Communists* (New York: Workers Library Publishers, 1938), p. 10.

15. N. Bukharin and E. Preobrazhensky, *The ABC of Communism: A Popular Explanation of the Program of the Communist Party of Russia,* trans. Eden and Paul Cedar (London: Communist Press of Britain, 1922), pp. 383–412.

16. *Ibid.,* p. 399.

17. *Ibid.,* p. 264.

18. The first document was published in Lenin, *Collected Works* (in Russian), 52: 140; the second in *Collected Works,* 54:440; emphases as in original. An English translation is in the Canadian (Communist) magazine, *The Marxist Quarterly,* no.˙ 17 (Spring 1966), p. 39.

19. Leslie Dewart, *Christianity and Revolution: The Lesson of Cuba* (New York: Herder & Herder, 1963).

Chapter 2. Openings

1. Thomas W. Ogletree, ed., *Openings for Marxist-Christian Dialogue* (Nashville: Abington Press, 1969).

2. Ibid., pp. 22–23.

3. Charles C. West, *Communism and the Theologians* (New York: Macmillan Co., 1963), p. 338.

4. Ogletree, *op. cit.,* pp. 23–24.

5. On the church in czarist Russia see John S. Curtiss, *Church and State in Russia* (New York: Octagon Books, 1965); on South Africa see Ernest Cole, with Thomas Flaherty, *House of Bondage* (New York: Random House, 1967), esp. pp. 150–67.

6. Fr. Giles Hibbert, "Socialism, Revolution and Christianity," *Labour Monthly* (London) 50 Dec. 1968): 561–62. That Fr. Hibbert chose to contribute to the leading

Marxist periodical in Britain is itself germane to our subject.

7. Ogletree, *op. cit.*, p. 331.

8. *Ibid.*, p. 24.

9. Marx, *Theses on Feuerbach*, no. 11.

10. World Council of Churches, *World Conference on Church and Society . . . Official Report* (Geneva: World Council of Churches, 1967), p. 201.

11. *Ibid.*, p. 208.

12. *Ibid.*, p. 206.

13. Ogletree, *op. cit.*, p. 24.

14. *Ibid.*, p. 25.

15. Palmiro Togliatti, "On International Working-Class Unity," *Political Affairs* 43, no. 10 (Oct. 1964): 44–45. First published in *Rinascita*, 5 Sept. 1964.

16. Ogletree, *op. cit.*, p. 26.

17. By no means entirely, of course. Thus West, in *Communism and the Theologians*, *op. cit.*, repeats this distortion. For numerous additional examples, see my *History and Reality* (New York: Cameron Associates, 1955), p. 26.

18. Ogletree, *op. cit.*, p. 32.

19. *Ibid.*, p. 37.

20. *Ibid.*, p. 39

21. The three quotations come from, respectively: Marx-Engels, *Correspondence, 1864–1895* (New York: International Publishers, n.d.), Engels to Schmidt, 8 Aug. 1890, p. 477; *Ibid.*, p. 473; F. Mehring, *Karl Marx* (New York: Covici, Friede, 1935), p. 238.

22. Ogletree, *op. cit.*, p. 41.

23. Homer W. Smith, *Man and His Gods*, foreword by Albert Einstein (New York: Grosset & Dunlap, 1957), pp. 228–29.

24. Ogletree, *op. cit.*, pp. 38, 45.

25. *Ibid.*, p. 30.

26. "Posterity," wrote Diderot, "is for the philosopher what the Other World is for the religious." And in the preface to the *Encyclopedia*, he explained his prodigious labors in affirming the hope "that we may not die without having deserved well of the human race." Such considerations certainly have been powerful motivations and remain so. The loss of confidence in any attractive future (or even *any* future!) is fundamental to the *malaise* so widespread today.

27. Compare the critique by Ogletree with that in my *History and Reality, op. cit.*, pp. 25, 125n.

Chapter 3. Widening the Opening

1. Thomas W. Ogletree, ed., *Openings for Marxist-Christian Dialogue* (Nashville: Abingdon Press, 1969).

2. *Ibid.*, pp. 52–53.

3. *Ibid.*, p. 57.

4. *Ibid.*, p. 62.

5. *Ibid.*, p. 63.

6. *Ibid.*, p. 67.

7. *Ibid.*, pp. 68–69.

8. Pierre Teilhard de Chardin, *The Phenomenon of Man* (New York: Harper Torchbooks, 1965), p. 224.

9. Ogletree, *op. cit.*, p. 69.

10. *Ibid.*, p. 71.

11. *Ibid.*, pp. 74–75.

12. *Ibid.*, p. 84.

13. West's footnote for this reads "Marx, *Collected Works*, XIII, 281"; but this is an obvious slip, as the reference should be to that volume of Lenin's *Collected Works*. The quotation is from Lenin, *Materialism and Empirio-Criticism* (1908). My quotations will be from the *Collected Works* (New York: International Publishers, 1927), vol. 13, since this is West's source.

14. Marx himself did not hesitate to call attention to what he thought were his own mistakes. Thus he drastically changed his view—taking, as he said, an opposite position from an earlier one—on the relationship between Irish emancipation and English working-class activity. See Marx's letter to Engels, London, 10 Dec. 1869. In their preface to the 1872 German edition of the *Communist Manifesto*, Marx and Engels declared that it was "in places out of date"; "especially" outdated, they said, was any idea of simply laying hold of the old bourgeois state and with it moving to socialism.

15. Ogletree, *op. cit.*, p. 116.

16. *Ibid.*, p. 120.

17. I have dealt with this question at some length in *The Nature of Democracy, Freedom and Revolution* (New York: International Publishers, 1967), esp. pp. 89–107.

18. Ogletree, *op. cit.*, pp. 130–31.

19. Barrington Moore, Jr., *Soviet Politics: The Dilemma of Power* (New York: Harper & Row, 1965), pp. 81–82.

20. Ogletree, *op. cit.*, p. 135.

21. I called attention to this and offered some suggestions in 1957 in *The Truth About Hungary* (New York: Mainstream Publishers, 1957), pp. 253–54. Note that by March 1922, Lenin was remarking that ". . . it is much easier to conquer power in a revolutionary epoch than to know how to use this power properly." ("On the Significance of Militant Materialism," in *Collected Works* [Moscow, 1966], 33: 229).

22. Ogletree, *op. cit.*, p. 140.

23. *Ibid.*, p. 142.

24. *Ibid.*, p. 150.

25. *Ibid.*, p. 167.

Chapter 4. Love and the Transcendental

1. Ralph Barton Perry, in Alexander Miller, *The Renewal of Man* (Garden City, N.Y.: Doubleday & Co., 1955), p. 43.

2. James W. Culliton, in *Business and Religion,* ed. Edward C. Bursk (New York: Harper & Row, 1958), p. 10. Morris R. Cohen pointed out that religion often seems to many Americans—as, for example, to Theodore Roosevelt—to be used "in an honorific sense, its old content or meaning is all gone, and we now apply it vaguely to any generous emotion, especially about social or political reform" (*American Thought: A Critical Sketch* [Glencoe, Ill.: Free Press, 1954], p. 227).

3. Alfred Bertholet, "Religion," *Encyclopedia of the Social Sciences* (New York: Macmillan Co., 1934), 13:229–30.

4. O. H. Ohmann, in *Business and Religion, op. cit.,* pp. 79-80.

5. George Sarton, in *Science, Religion and Reality,* ed. Joseph Needham (New York: Braziller, 1955), p. 5.

6. Marx, in *Karl Marx: Early Writings,* ed. T. B. Bottomore (New York: McGraw-Hill, 1964), p. 9. The Gallup Poll of December 1968 on the question of religiousness showed that "the proportion of adults who attend church in a typical week is greater in the U.S. than in ten other nations of the Western world" and that "the percentage of Americans who say they believe in God, in an after-life and in hell far exceeds the percentages with such beliefs in eleven other nations" (*New York Times,* 22, 26 Dec. 1968.

7. Guerva Banyres, in Libero Pierantozzi, "Social Doctrine of the Vatican and the 20th Century," *World Marxist Review,* July 1965.

8. Hayim Greenberg, in Nahum N. Glatzer, *The Dimensions of Job: A Study and Selected Readings* (New York: Schocken Books, 1969), p. 223. Frederick J. Adelmann, S.J., of Boston College writes of faith: "one does not get it by proofs from reason, nor does it depend on scientific evidence." And as to evil: "There is still a great mystery here that has its full answer hidden in divine providence ..." (*From Dialogue to Epilogue* [The Hague: Martinus Nijhoff, 1968], pp. 53, 58.

9. Marvin H. Pope, *The Anchor Bible* (Garden City, N.Y.: Doubleday Anchor Books, 1965), intro. to Job.

10. Frederick Buechner, "Despair in the Final Hour," *The Christian Century,* 12 Mar. 1969.

11. Albert Einstein, in Philipp Frank, *Einstein: His Life and Times* (New York: Alfred A. Knopf, 1947), p. 284.

12. Michael Verret, "On Love and Marxism," *The Marxist Quarterly* (Toronto), no. 17 (Apr. 1966).

13. Gustav A. Wetter, *Dialectical Materialism* (New York: Praeger, 1963), p. 552.

14. John Lewis, in *Christianity and the Social Revolution,* eds. J. Lewis, K. Polanyi, and D. Kitchin (London: Gollancz, 1935), p. 500. It must be noted that Father Wetter attempts to make Lenin's descriptions and definitions of matter also almost tactical rather than fundamental. But to do this, it is necessary for him to

quote Lenin as writing: "Nature is infinite" without completing the sentence: "Nature is infinite, but it infinitely *exists.*" The addition is crucial, for as Lenin writes: "For the sole 'property' of matter with whose recognition philosophical materialism is bound up is the property of *being an objective reality,* of existing outside our mind." See Wetter, *op. cit.,* p. 288; Lenin, *Materialism and Empirio-Criticism* (Moscow: Foreign Languages Publishing House, n.d.), pp. 269, 271. See also Arthur Gibson, *The Faith of an Atheist* (New York: Harper & Row, 1968), pp. 115–17; and Daniel Goldstick, "On the Dialectical Unity of the Marxist Concept of Matter," *Horizons* (Toronto), no. 28, (Winter 1969).

15. Alfred Stiernotte, "Mysticism and Communism," *Journal for the Scientific Study of Religion* 6 (1967): 112.

16. The literature on Teilhard is already massive. See especially Claude Cuénot and Roger Garaudy, *Science and Faith in Teilhard de Chardin* (London: Garnstone Press, 1969), and, of his own writings, *The Phenomenon of Man,* intro. Julian Huxley (New York: Harper Torchbooks, 1961).

Chapter 5. Ethics and Humanity

1. Vernon Venable, *Human Nature: The Marxian View* (New York: Alfred A. Knopf, 1945), pp. 163–64.

2. John Middleton Murry, *Heroes of Thought* (New York: Julian Messner, 1938), p. 336.

3. Friedrich Engels, *Anti-Dühring* (New York: International Publishers, n.d.), p. 108. Insofar as Joseph Fletcher's "situation ethics" reflects time, place, and condition, it is an advance over an abstracted and dogmatic ethical outlook. But his own presentation suffers from application only to the subjective and the individual. As he himself writes, affirming the validity of such criticism, ". . . I must next prepare an analysis of situation theory as a method for social ethics, showing some of its practical uses and results" (in *The Situation Ethics Debate,* ed. Harvey Cox [Philadelphia: Westminster Press, 1968], p. 262).

4. Anthony Downs, formerly of the University of Chicago and a member of the National Commission on Urban Problems, writes: "Thousands of infants are attacked by rats each year; hundreds die or become mentally retarded from eating lead paint that falls from cracked walls; thousands more are ill because of unsanitary conditions resulting from jamming large families into a single room, [the] continuing failure of landlords to repair plumbing or provide proper heat . . ." (in *Agenda for the Nation,* ed. Kermit Gordon [Washington: Brookings Inst., 1968], p. 42. Sandra Blakeslee, reporting on a conference held by five organizations related to housing, said the findings included the fact that "Lead poisoning, which can lead to chronic illness, brain damage or death, affects *tens of thousands* of American youngsters each year who live in slum housing" (italics added). Most of the victims are under five years of age (*The New York Times,* 27 Mar. 1969).

5. In Marx and Engels, *The First Indian War of Independence* (Moscow: Foreign Languages Publishing House, n.d.), p. 91.

6. Horace Davis, *Nationalism & Socialism: Marxist and Labor Theories of Nationalism to 1917* (New York: Monthly Review Press, 1967), p. 60.

7. First published in the *New York Daily Tribune*, 8 Aug. 1853; in Marx and Engels, *op. cit.*, p. 38.

8. In addition to the previously cited source (*ibid.*), see the larger collection, Marx and Engels, *On Colonialism* (Moscow, 1968), which has material not only on India but also on China, Persia, Ireland, Burma, and elsewhere.

9. Paul Oestreicher, "Opening to the East," *The Center Magazine*, May 1969, p. 30.

10. Quentin Lauer, S.J., "The Status of Marxist-Christian Dialogue," *Ave Maria*, 12 Apr: 1969, p. 29.

11. See especially F. R. Tennant, *The Source of the Doctrines of the Fall and Original Sin*, trans. Mary F. Thelen (New York: Schocken Books, 1968), originally published in 1903. On "original sin" and the differences concerning it between Judaism and Christianity, see Leo Baeck, *The Essence of Judaism* (New York: Schocken Books, 1961), esp. p. 162.

12. In Marx and Engels, *The Holy Family* (Moscow: Foreign Languages Publishing House, 1956), pp. 175–76.

13. Marx, *Capital* (New York: International Publishers, 1967), I:196n.

14. The fact that in slavery in the United States the relative absence of fluid capital impeded investment in machinery in general, as well as in improving methods of production, is quite beside the point of the present discussion; indeed, its absence at this point in Marx's writings adds to the force of the above comment. Benjamin Farrington believed that similar considerations of a subjective nature decisively influenced mechanical developments in ancient slavery; see his "Prometheus Bound: Government and Science in Classical Antiquity," *Science and Society* II (Fall 1938): 441–43.

15. Primo Levi, *Survival in Auschwitz* (New York: Collier Books, 1961), p. 36.

16. Marx, *Economic and Philosophic Manuscripts, 1844* (Moscow: Foreign Languages Publishing House, 1961), pp. 72–73, 75, 105.

17. Engels, *Outlines of a Critique of Political Economy*, an appendix to the *Economic and Philosophic Manuscripts, 1844, op. cit.*, p. 177.

18. Marx, *Critique of Hegel's Philosophy of Law* (1843); see Loyd D. Easton and Kurt H. Guddat, eds. and trans., *Writings of the Young Marx on Philosophy and Society* (Garden City, N.Y.: Doubleday & Co., 1967), pp. 257–58.

19. Roger Garaudy, "The Marxist-Christian Dialogue ...," *The Marxist Quarterly* (Toronto), no. 17 (April 1966), pp. 13–14.

20. Marx, *Critique of Hegel's Philosophy of Law, op. cit.*, p. 257.

21. See my *History and Reality* (New York: Cameron Associates, 1955), pp. 26–27.

22. Engels, *Outlines of a Critique of Political Economy, op. cit.*, p. 209.

23. Marx, *Capital, op. cit.*, I:759–60.

24. Engels, *The Condition of the Working Class in England in 1844*, trans. Florence Kelley Wischnewetzky (New York, 1887), pp. 20, 24, 32.

25. Engels, *Condition of the Working Class, op. cit.,* pp. 17–18, 116–17. The slumbering and suppressed powers anticipated by some generations Harvey Cox's denunciation of "sloth" and his apt insistence that this, rather than the much-emphasized "sin" of pride, has been a major human affliction. I would add that insofar as "sloth" represents a deliberate curtailing of the human potential, it has been aimed more against women than against men. See Cox, *On Not Leaving It to the Snake* (New York: Macmillan Co., 1967), intro.

26. John Lewis, in *What Kind of Revolution?,* eds. J. Klugmann and P. Oestreicher (London: Panther, 1968), p. 22. I agree with John Somerville that "It is well nigh incredible that philosophically experienced commentators have sometimes pronounced Marxism to be an amoral system" ("Marxist Ethics, Determinism and Freedom," *Philosophy & Phenomenological Research* 28 [1965]: 22).

27. In Marx and Engels, *Selected Works, in One Volume* (New York: International Publishers, 1968), p. 273.

28. On the question of inevitability, see in particular G. Plekhanov, *Fundamental Problems of Marxism* (New York: International Publishers, 1969), pp. 93–102, 139–177; John Somerville, *Methodology in Social Science* (New York, 1938), p. 66; Somerville, *Soviet Philosophy* (New York, 1946), p. 93; and Aptheker, *History and Reality, op. cit.,* pp. 33–37.

29. See the many articles on these authors in *Marxism Today* (London) from 1967 through 1969; in particular, see critiques from varying scientific disciplines collected by M. F. Ashley Montagu, ed., *Man and Aggression* (London: Oxford University Press, 1968).

30. For the merest sampling of such expression, see my "On the Superiority of the Negro," *American Dialog,* Oct.-Nov. 1965, pp. 33–36. Indicative of this strand in Jewish thought is Richard C. Hertz, *What Can a Man Believe?* (New York: Bloch Publishers, 1967), esp. p. 27.

31. Thomas Jefferson, in Herbert Aptheker, *American Negro Slave Revolts* (New York, 1943), pp. 219–24.

32. John Rhodes, in *Business and Religion,* ed. Edward C. Bursk (New York: Harper & Row, 1958), pp. 87–88.

33. Robert Kysar, a professor of religion at Hamline University, St. Paul, Minnesota, suggests that "debate over belief in God ... has reached a stalemate." He thinks it might well be dropped and that focus be placed on the "one value in common: concern for the quality of human existence" ("Toward a Common Humanism," *The Christian Century,* 21 May 1969, p. 706).

Chapter 6. Reason and Religion

1. D. B. Runcorn, vicar of St. Mary's Shortlands, Bromley, England, makes the temptation into one that was "to acquire the private ownership of the means of production." While this would be convenient in terms of Marxist-religious convergence, it does seem to be a dubious reading of the Bible. In J. Klugmann, *Dialogue of Christianity and Marxism* (London, 1968), p. 49.

2. Hayim Greenberg, "The Inner Eye," (1940), in Nahum N. Glatzer, *The Di-*

mensions of Job: A Study and Selected Readings (New York: Schocker Books, 1969), p. 224.

3. Arthur C. Cochrane, "Joy to the World: The Message of Ecclesiastes," *The Christian Century*, 18 Dec. 1968, pp. 1596–98.

4. Thomas Hooker, "The Activity of Faith," in *Theology in America. . .* , ed. S. E. Ahlstrom (Indianapolis: Bobbs-Merrill, 1967), p. 135.

5. Gnosticism tended to reject the denunciation of reason, but it was harried for generations as a dangerous heresy. This was especially true of the Ophite sect; they accepted the gnostic ideas of the complete separation of spirit from matter and the creation of the world by an inferior God, the Demiurge. For God could have no direct contact with matter, and attainment of salvation was through knowledge. They added reverence for the serpent (hence their name) as Adam's assistant, who, by opening the way to knowledge, opened the way to salvation. In the fifth and sixth centuries the Ophites were severely penalized; see Constance I. Smith, "Ophites and Fathers," *Journal of the History of Ideas* 30 (Apr.-May 1969): 249–50. The Manichee also held to the idea that the world was made by a lesser God—indeed, by Satan. This view was a significant element in religious history for a thousand years, especially in Persia and the farther East. Graham Greene writes of "the eternal and alluring taint of the Manichee, with its simple and terrible explanation of our plight, how the world was made by Satan and not by God . . ." (*Collected Essays* [London: Bodley Head, 1969]).

6. Thomas Aquinas, *The Summa Theologica of Saint Thomas Aquinas,* 2 vols. (Chicago: Encyclopaedia Britannica, 1952), I:5, II:333, 393. Franz Schurmann observes that in China the view was dominantly "common-sensical." The Chinese, he adds, "didn't even believe in God who, in other cultures, is a legitimate source of irrationality" (*New York Review of Books* [15 Dec. 1968], p. 3). The late Dr. D. B. Krishna of India notes that while "Christianity is theistic, Buddhism is agnostic. It denies the existence of soul. It openly confesses its ignorance of God." He also wrote that "it extolled reason as a determining criterion of belief. . . . It was primarily a religion of conduct, not a religion of observances. . . ." Hence, "it maintained an attitude of dynamic social action . . . a collective revolutionary attitude" (*Political and Social Thought of the Buddhist Writers of the Early Christian Era* [Delhi, 1960], pp. 98, 103, 105).

7. Nathaniel W. Taylor, in *Theology in America. . .* , *op. cit.,* pp. 222-23.

8. Charles P. Krauth, *The Conservative Reformation and Its Theology* (Philadelphia: Lippincott, 1871).

9. Sydney E. Ahlstrom remarks: "Nonrecognition of Hodge's continuing role in American Protestantism betokens a serious misunderstanding of the contemporary scene" (*Theology in America. . .* , *op. cit.,* p. 252). Eerdmans continues to publish five of his works; as late as 1952 it reprinted the three volumes of *Systematic Theology.*

10. On Claude Williams, who at this writing continues his literally Christ-like mission in the South, see Cedric Belfrage, *A Faith to Free the People* (New York: Dryden Press, 1944).

11. What George Dering Wolff was writing in the United States was being written

internationally in the same period. Thus Pope Pius IX, in his *Syllabus errorum*, a list of eighty errors appended to the encyclical *Quanta Cura* (1864), condemned naturalism and rationalism, socialism and communism; the final error condemned was the concept that "the Pope of Rome could and should arrive at a conciliation and agreement with progress, liberalism and modern culture." In the Dutch periodical *De Katholiek*, Father Robert Adolfs has told us that in 1880 it was stated: "the social question springs from a political conspiracy. . . . The solution to the prevailing unrest lies in *contentedness*, the contented spirits with which the working people must bear their lot, because they are Christians. The last word on the social question is the kindly disposition of the better sort of persons and the charity which their love disposes them to exercise" (*The Church Is Different* [New York: Harper & Row, 1966], originally published in Dutch in 1964).

12. Jan M. Lochman, "Christianity and Marxism: Convergence and Divergence," *Christianity and Crisis*, 12 May 1969, pp. 131–33. Lochman, a professor of theology and philosophy at the Comenius Faculty of Theology in Prague, is the Harry Emerson Fosdick Visiting Professor at the Union Theological Seminary during 1969–70.

Chapter 7. Sex, Women, and Religion

1. Joseph Wood Krutch, "Modern Love and Modern Fiction," in *Our Changing Morality*, ed. Freda Kirchway (New York: Boni, 1930), p. 173.

2. The primitive Christian idea involved the resurrection of the body; the dogma of the immortality of the soul appears later. In *Le Livre de Job* (1859), Ernest Renan noted that the two concepts have "never been reconciled in a very natural manner"; the difficulty persists to this day and one of its manifestations is the funeral service, the preparation of the deceased, and the prayers said over the corpse. Oscar Cullman finds resurrection to be the unique witness of the New Testament in *Immortality of the Soul or Resurrection of the Dead?* (London: Epworth, 1958). For an essay on the remaining confusions as shown in funeral practices, see B. H. Throckmorton, Jr., "Do Christians Believe in Death?," *The Christian Century*, 21 May 1969, pp. 708–10. In 1869 a rabbinical conference in Philadelphia representing Reform Judaism passed this Resolution: "The belief in the resurrection of the body has no religious foundation [in Judaism] and the doctrine of immortality refers to the after-existence of the soul only." That many Jews differ is indicated in the ferocity of the campaign waged against permitting autopsies in Israel. The 1869 Resolution is in Richard C. Hertz, *What Can a Man Believe* (New York: Bloch Publishers, 1967), p. 93.

3. Christian writing specifically objecting to the identity of sex with sin is not wanting, of course. Notable in this connection is the nineteenth-century Russian, V. Rozanov. See C. S. Calian, *Berdyaev's Philosophy of Hope* (Minneapolis: Augsburg, 1969), p. 21.

4. Bertrand Russell, "Our Changing Morality," in *Our Changing Morality*, *op. cit.*, pp. 3–4.

5. See Henry Sidgwick, *Outlines of the History of Ethics* (London: Macmillan & Co., 1925), p. 125n.

6. For these and other illustrations, see the excellent work by Mary Daly, *The Church and the Second Sex* (New York: Harper & Row, 1968). It should be added that Ambrose continued in condemnation of "the seductiveness of youth"; the relationship of youth with sexuality and the tendency toward denunciation of the young in much of religion would be worthy of a book of its own.

7. An ancient Russian proverb goes: "A hen is no bird, a woman—no human."

8. Mary Daly reports that two women correspondents were barred from a ceremony in the Sistine Chapel in May 1966. An Italian bishop explained to the ladies: "This is for the Pope a special day. We must not allow a woman to sully the Sistine Chapel for His Holiness" (*op. cit.*, p. 99). The fourth edition of the *Dictionary of Moral Theology* (Rome, 1969) declares under its section "Sexual Equality": "This equality is purely Utopian, seeing as how it has no biological basis whatsoever and simply tends to ensure the complete economic and social independence of women. . . . We must hope for the return of women to the industrious, healthy, and serene peace of domestic life, far from the cares, the struggles, and the anxieties which are characteristic of masculine activities." Adultery is held to be more serious when committed by women than by men "because (especially when committed with several men) it can bring on sterility." In the same work, an article by Cardinal Felici warns that undergoing Freudian analysis is, probably, a mortal sin. The *Dictionary* announces that it was revised "in the light of Vatican Council II." (Quotations from *Commonweal*, 21 Feb. 1969, p. 630).

9. George A. Kelly, *Catholic Marriage Manual* (New York: Random House, 1956), p. 6.

10. In Sally Cunneen, *Sex: Female; Religion: Catholic* (New York: Holt, Rinehart, & Winston, 1968).

11. Barbara Welter, "The Cult of True Womanhood," *American Quarterly* 18, no. 2, pt. 1 (Summer 1966): 151–74.

12. Ralph Waldo Emerson, "Woman," in *Complete Writings* (New York, 1875), p. 1180; Nathaniel Hawthorne, *The Blithedale Romance* (Boston, 1852), p. 71. English law held that a woman who killed her husband was guilty of "petty treason"; the penalty was death by fire. This law was not repealed until 1790.

13. E. L. Thorndike, "Sex in Education," *Bookman*, April 1906. Readers will have discerned the marked similarity between descriptions of women and descriptions of colored peoples, especially the American Negro. Note that arguments about their educability and the kinds of education "most suited" for them are also strikingly similar. For example, Thorndike is writing of women's education as above at the very same time that the dispute concerning Negro education, typified by Washington vs. Du Bois, was at its height.

14. See Sylvia Kopald, "Where Are the Female Geniuses?," in *Our Changing Morality, op. cit.*, pp. 107–8.

15. In Germany, if a woman gave birth to a daughter in a hospital, it was customary for the father not to visit the wife; if a son, he would visit. In the German

Democratic Republic, if such behavior persisted, a committee would visit the father and attempt to convince thim that his behavior was boorish and backward; as often as not the committee succeeded only in arousing curses. Now, when a father calls to learn the sex of his child, he is simply told "a child." He must visit his wife at the hospital if he wishes more specifics. This seems to work better than the committee method.

16. Lenin, *Collected Works* (Moscow: Progresss Publishers, 1964), 23:329.

Chapter 8. Racism and Religion

1. Francis B. Simkins, *The South Old and New: A History, 1820–1947* (New York: Alfred A. Knopf, 1947), p. 83.

2. See in particular David B. Davis, *The Problem of Slavery in Western Culture* (Ithaca, N.Y.: Cornell University Press, 1966); and, with important additions, Louis Ruchames, "The Sources of Racial Thought in Colonial America," *Journal of Negro History* 52 (Oct. 1967): 251–72. Two older works that are still valuable are: R. W. Logan, "The Attitude of the Church Toward Slavery Prior to 1500," *Journal of Negro History* 17 (Oct. 1932): 472ff., and R. W. and A. J. Carlyle, *A History of Medieval Political Thought in the West* (London: Cambridge University Press, 1927).

3. Davis, *op. cit.*, p. 89.

4. *Ibid.*, p. 194.

5. W. S. Jenkins, *Pro-Slavery Thought in the Old South* (Chapel Hill, N.C.: University of North Carolina Press, 1935), p. 254.

6. This sermon is presented in full in *The Burden of Race*, ed. Gilbert Osofsky (New York: Harper & Row, 1967), pp. 39 ff.

7. Herbert Aptheker, *American Negro Slave Revolts* (New York: Columbia University Press, 1943), pp. 56–57. (This should be read within the context of its chapter, "The Machinery of Control," pp. 53–78).

8. Charles S. Davis, *The Cotton Kingdom in Alabama* (Montgomery, 1939), p. 89.

9. I. A. Newby, *Jim Crow's Defense: Anti-Negro Thought in America, 1900–1930* (Baton Rouge: Louisiana State University Press, 1965), p. 85; Robert M. Miller, "The Attitudes of American Protestantism Towards the Negro, 1919–1929," *Journal of Negro History* 41 (July 1956): 215. For the story in its entirety, see F. S. Loescher, *The Protestant Church and the Negro* (New York: Association Press, 1948).

10. W. E. B. Du Bois, in *The Crisis* 30 (July 1925): 121; David H. Pierce, in *The Crisis* 30 (Aug. 1925): 184–86.

11. See W. H. and J. H. Pease, eds., *The Anti-Slavery Argument* (Indianapolis: Bobbs-Merrill, 1965), esp. pp. 111–42; Aptheker, "The Quakers and Negro Slavery," in *Toward Negro Freedom* (New York: New Century, 1956), pp. 10–35; T. E. Drake, *Quakers and Slavery in America* (New Haven: Yale University Press, 1950);

B. Forbush, *Elias Hicks, Quaker Liberal* (New York: Columbia University Press, 1956). See also Frederick Douglass' exposition of the antislavery record of early Methodism in a speech delivered in 1855 in Rochester, N.Y., in *Life and Writings of Douglass*, ed. P. S. Foner, 4 vols. (New York, 1950), II p. 338.

12. In *The Christian Century*, 12 June 1968, p. 803.

13. Dispatch from Gloria Emerson, *New York Times*, 22 May 1969.

14. Du Bois, *The Autobiography of W. E. B. Du Bois* (New York: International Publishers, 1968), pp. 42–43. He also writes that "the Negro Church arose as the center and almost the only social expression of Negro life in America" (*Black Folk: Then and Now* [New York: Henry Holt & Co., 1939], p. 198). Compare Carter G. Woodson: "The Negro church, in short, has served as a clearing house for the community" (*The History of the Negro Church* [Washington: Associated Publishers, 1921], p. 272). A rather lengthy and sympathetic analysis of the Negro church by Du Bois is in his little-known article, "The Problem of Amusement," *The College Settlement News* (Philadelphia) 3, no. 6 (Oct. 1897). (This paper is located in the Smith College Library, Northampton, Massachusetts.)

15. Aptheker, ed., *A Documentary History of the Negro People in the United States* (New York: Citadel Press, 1951), p. 205.

16. *Life and Writings of Douglass, op. cit.*, 2:196 ff.

17. Du Bois, in Du Bois and Booker T. Washington, *The Negro in the South* (Philadelphia: Jacobs, 1907), p. 177. For evidence of similar distinctions between white Christianity—passivity and heavenly reward—and black Christianity—activity and freedom on earth—in the West Indies, see Mary Reckord, "The Jamaica Slave Rebellion of 1831," *Past & Present*, no. 40 (July 1968), pp. 108–25.

18. Channing Phillips, address before International Conference on Racism sponsored by the World Council of Churches, London, 21 May 1969; reported in the *New York Times*, 22 May 1969.

19. On the groundwork of elitism, consider traditional views about women's "nature," or what royalty thought of peasants, or what the masters thought of slaves in ancient days, when racism was not present. On the last item, Davis comments: "Throughout history it has been said that slaves, though occasionally as loyal and faithful as good dogs, were for the most part lazy, irresponsible, cunning, rebellious, untrustworthy, and sexually promiscuous" (*op. cit.*, pp. 59–60). Generally the idea has held that the poor are poor because they are no good; witness the dual meaning of poor and of rich.

20. Note that the Social Gospel movement in the United States, especially from about 1890 until World War I, almost totally ignored the condition of black people when it was particularly awful with literally dozens of lynchings reported each month. When it was not ignored, expressions of a more or less blatantly racist character appeared. See Thomas F. Gossett, *Race: The History of an Idea in America* (Dallas: Southern Methodist University Press, 1963), chap. 8; and Robert T. Handy, ed., *The Social Gospel in America: Gladden, Ely, Rauschenbusch* (New York: Oxford University Press, 1966), pp. 29–30.

21. See in particular the work of the Afro-American Communist leader, Claude

NOTES

Lightfoot, *Ghetto Rebellion to Black Liberation* (New York: International Publishers, 1968), esp. pp. 139–82.

Chapter 9. Life, Death, and Religion

1. Roger Garaudy, in *The Christian-Marxist Dialogue*, ed. Paul Oestreicher (New York: Macmillan Co., 1969), p. 146.

2. John Calvin, *Institutes*, 3:ix, 4.

3. Corliss Lamont, *The Illusion of Immortality*, 3rd ed. rev. (New York: Philosophical Library, 1959).

4. William James, *The Varieties of Religious Experience* (New York: Longmans, 1910), p. 524; Milton McC. Gatch, *Death: Meaning and Mortality in Christian Thought and Contemporary Culture* (New York: Seabury Press, 1969), p. 15.

5. Gatch, *op. cit.*, p. 16.

6. Efforts to create life and to overcome death are progressing in laboratories throughout the world. The former is closer to accomplishment than the latter, and the latter is no longer inconceivable. See a popular presentation: V. Pekelis, "Can We Kill Death?," *Sputnik* (Moscow), Feb. 1969, pp. 90–93. Medical advances already require fresh definitions of death and reconsideration of questions of prolonging life; see the Report of the Committee of the Harvard Medical School, *Journal of the American Medical Association*, Aug. 5, 1968.

7. Gatch, *op. cit.*, pp. 184, 187.

8. Lamont, *op. cit.*, p. 278.

9. Lenin, *Collected Works* (Moscow: Foreign Languages Publishing House, 1963), 16:363. A Marxist tends to agree with Spinoza: "There is nothing over which a free man ponders less than death; his wisdom is to meditate not on death but on life." Therein lies a major difference between Marxism and (most) religions.

10. Ilya Metchnikoff, *The Prolongation of Life* (New York: G. P. Putnam, 1908).

11. Walter Savage Landor, "Dying Speech of an Old Philosopher." See Lamont, *op. cit.*, pp. 209–10.

12. W. E. B. Du Bois, in Aptheker, "On the Passing of Du Bois," *Political Affairs*, Oct. 1963, pp. 40–41.

13. Marx and Engels, *Selected Works: In One Volume* (New York: International Publishers, 1968), pp. 435–36.

14. Samuel Hugo Bergman, *Faith and Reason: An Introduction to Modern Jewish Thought*, trans. Alfred Jospe (New York: Schocken Books, 1966), pp. 112–13. This is related to the distortion that makes Marxism view history-making as independent of man, as "For the orthodox Communist there is an inner logic in history which is not dependent on man . . ." (Harvey Cox, *The Secular City* [New York: Macmillan Co., 1965], p. 68). For a Marxist to speak of history as independent of man is a contradiction in terms. In a later work, Cox does not affirm this reading of Marxism as a fact but puts it in the form of a question, saying "Marxism remains unclear on this point." It is not Marxism that is unclear on this point; it is Cox who is in the

process of making up his mind. See his *On Leaving It to the Snake* (New York: Macmillan Co., 1967), pp. 86–87.

15. See my *History and Reality* (New York: Cameron Associates, 1955) and *Laureates of Imperialism* (New York: Masses & Mainstream, 1954); Max Horkheimer, *The Eclipse of Reason* (New York: Oxford University Press, 1947); Paul A. Carter, *The Idea of Progress in American Protestant Thought, 1930–1960* (Philadelphia: Fortress Press, 1969).

16. For the intellectual striving of one so affected, see Richard L. Rubenstein, "Auschwitz and Covenant Theology," *The Christian Century*, 21 May 1969, pp. 716–18.

17. Trans. by Robert G. Colodny from Lázaro Somoza-Silva, *El General Miaja: Biografiá de un Heroe* (Mexico City, 1944), p. 183; to appear in full in Colodny, *Spain: The Glory and the Tragedy* (New York: Humanities Press, to be pub.).

Chapter 10. Marxism, Religion, and Revolution

1. For even more recent, more extended, and more dramatic evidence of the universality of the comprehension of the special crisis afflicting American society, see *Agenda for the Nation*, ed. Kermit Gordon (Washington: Brookings Inst., 1968). This contains eighteen essays on domestic and foreign affairs by distinguished political and academic figures; all revolve around deepening crisis and all agree on seeing no viable solution, given the present social structure. My analysis of the volume appears in two parts in *Political Affairs*, May and June 1969.

2. Herbert W. Richardson, *Toward an American Theology* (New York: Harper & Row, 1967).

3. Vittorio Lanternari, *The Religions of the Oppressed*, trans. Lisa Sergio (New York: Alfred A. Knopf, 1965), first published in Rome in 1960.

4. Christ was bringing "good news to the poor" (Luke 4:18); Jesus said, "You cannot serve God and mammon" (Matthew 6:24); the New Testament teaches, "The love of money is the root of all evil" (I Timothy 6:10); the Rule of St. Benedict ordered "the vice of private ownership" to be "cut off . . . by the roots," and so on. A contemporary reassertion of this revolutionary kernel is in Martin A. Marty, *The Search for a Usable Future* (New York: Harper & Row, 1969), p. 109: "Christians cannot, however, fulfill their missions and mandates without coming to some sort of terms with that aspect of life covered by the term revolution or radical social change. The alternative is to put oneself a priori on the side of the status quo, no matter how evil and dehumanizing it may be. In that instance, it would be hard to picture Christians speaking at all of the future of man. They have then opted for stagnation, slavery, and death."

5. The verbatim record is conveniently at hand in Jacques Zeller, *Christian Beginnings* (New York: Hawthorn Books, 1960), pp. 177–80.

6. See Philip Berrigan, S.S.J., *A Punishment for Peace* (New York: Macmillan Co., 1969), pp. 171–74.

7. Originally published in the French Catholic review, *Lettre,* Dec. 1964; in translation, in *Political Affairs,* June 1965.

8. See the *New Statesman* (London), 24 Mar. 1967, and Nino Lo Bello, *The Vatican Empire* (New York: Trident Press, 1968).

9. Alfred Blake, *The Religion Business* (Richmond, Va.: John Knox Press, 1968).

10. Robert Sherrill, in *Mayday* (Washington), no. 17 (3–10 Feb. 1969), p. 3.

11. Mortimer M. Caplan, as quoted by Edward B. Fiske in the *New York Times,* 2 Mar. 1969.

12. Harvey Cox, in *Christianity and Crisis,* 9 Dec. 1968, p. 295.

13. Blake, *op. cit.,* p. 28. Harvey Cox writes: "The American church has at least as much of a vested interest in the present structure of the American economy and society as the medieval church had in feudalism or the prerevolutionary Catholic churches of Eastern Europe had in private property ... it is dependent on the economy for its institutional life ..." (*The Secular City* [New York: Macmillan Co., 1965], p. 234).

14. The priests' action is described by George Dugan, *New York Times,* 27 Mar. 1969. The resolution of the United Presbyterian Church is in Blake, *op. cit.,* pp. 65–66. Important data are in D. B. Robertson, *Should Churches Be Taxed?* (Philadelphia: Westminster Press, 1968), esp. chap. 7. Very recently the National Council of Churches and the U.S. Catholic Conference asked Congress to eliminate the special exemption churches enjoy from income taxes on unrelated business income; see the *New York Times,* 3 May 1969.

15. Arthur O. Lovejoy, "The Communism of St. Ambrose," *Journal of the History of Ideas* 3 (1942): 458–68. It is relevant to point out that while *The Columbia Encyclopedia* (1950 ed.) finds space in its account of Ambrose to mention the number of hymns that he wrote, it makes no mention of this aspect of his thought.

16. Anthony Towne, "Revolution and the Marks of Baptism," *Journal of the Committee of Southern Churchmen,* Summer 1967.

17. Helder Camara, in *Social Revolution in the New Latin America: A Catholic Appraisal,* ed. J. J. Considine (Notre Dame, Ind.: University of Notre Dame Press, 1966), preface. (The whole book is really to my point.) Archbishop Camara also stated: "I am against violence. But I do not condemn those priests, like Camilo Torres, who have chosen violence. I understand them." In November 1967 he proclaimed the Communist Che Guevara a "martyr of America" (in Roque Dalton, "Catholics and Communists in Latin America," *World Marxist Review,* Jan. 1968, p. 86n.).

18. Tissa Belasuriya, in *Cross Currents,* Winter 1967, p. 56.

19. See the report by Mortimer Arias of the Latin American Ecumenical Encounter, held in Uruguay in December 1967, and published in *The Christian Century,* 28 Feb. 1968.

20. *Los Angeles Times,* 11 Feb. 1968.

21. The full text of the bishops' message is in *Catholic Mind,* Jan. 1968.

22. See Eula K. Long, "Priests with Pricked Consciences," *The Christian Century,* 17 Jan. 1968. For a fairly conservative presentation of basic data on Latin America, see the two-volume UNESCO work, *Social Aspects of Economic Develop-*

THE URGENCY OF MARXIST-CHRISTIAN DIALOGUE

ment in Latin America, ed. Egbert De Vries, et al. (1960).

23. Bishop Jorge Marcos de Oliveira, quoted in "News and Views," *Commonweal,* 9 Feb. 1968. In the spring of 1968, a 28-year-old priest-teacher, Father Henrique Pereira Neto, assistant to Archbishop Camara, was found hanging from a tree on the campus of the University of Recife with three bullet wounds in his head. The Archbishop led a funeral procession of 5,000; all pledged to continue "the struggle for the material and spiritual liberation of our people" (*The Christian Century,* 18 June 1969, p. 834).

24. Dispatch from Malcolm W. Browne in Buenos Aires, *New York Times,* 21 Apr. 1968.

25. Quoted from and commented upon editorially in *The Christian Century,* 19 Feb. 1969. Part of the explanation for the movement within Catholicism in Latin America may lie in the very rapid growth of Protestantism there; all South America counted about 100,000 Protestants in 1920, while in 1969 the count numbered about 4,600,000. For evidences of radicalism among them, see the account of the Latin American Ecumenical Encounter in Uraguay in December 1967 in *The Christian Century,* 28 Feb. 1968.

26. Quoted from and summarized editorially in *The Christian Century,* 5 Mar. 1969.

27. Dispatch from Malcolm W. Browne in Concepción, *New York Times,* 9 May 1969. The magazine, *America,* noted with some concern that the Uruguayan Catholic journal, *Vispera,* had published an article in October 1968 entitled "Christ Was Not a Property Owner," and stating, "Christ spoke very clearly, and the capitalist system totally contradicts what He said" (8 Mar. 1969, p. 267).

28. Dispatch from Tad Szulc in Madrid, *New York Times,* 8 Mar. 1968. One is reminded of Keynes's remark: "Modern capitalism is absolutely irreligious," in R. H. Tawney, *Religion and the Rise of Capitalism* (New York: Harcourt, Brace, 1926), p. 286.

29. Charles Abrams, *The City Is the Frontier* (New York: Harper & Row, 1965); Hans Blumenfeld, *The Modern Metropolis* (Cambridge: M.I.T. Press, 1968); Martin Luther King, Jr., *Where Do We Go from Here?* (New York: Harper & Row, 1967); and, for example, R. K. Taylor, "Property Rights and Human Rights," *The Christian Century,* 6 Sept. 1967. See also Anthony Downs, "Moving Toward Realistic Housing Goals," in *Agenda for the Nation, op. cit.,* pp. 142–78.

30. Figures cited by TRB in *The New Republic,* 3 May 1969.

31. Fr. James Groppi, "The Church and Civil Disobedience," *Motive,* Feb. 1969, pp. 43, 47.

32. Rev. James Gunther, quoted by Bill Kovach, *New York Times,* 4 Apr. 1969.

33. A useful summary of Vatican thinking and acting in the area of social concern is Richard L. Camp, *The Papal Ideology of Social Reform: A Study in Historical Development, 1878–1967* (Leiden: E. J. Brill, 1969). It is intensely anti-Communist, which will not make it less persuasive for most Americans.

34. Juan Luis Segundo, S.J. (of Uruguay), in *Christianity and Crisis,* 4 Mar. 1968, p. 31.

35. The *Book Review* feature was devoted to Herbert Marcuse, 10 Mar. 1968.

NOTES

36. Michael Novak, in *Commonweal*, 14 July 1967.

37. Julian N. Hartt, *A Christian Critique of American Culture* (New York: Harper & Row, 1967), p. 422.

38. Loyd D. Easton and Kurt H. Guddat, eds. and trans., *Writings of the Young Marx on Philosophy and Society* (Garden City, N.Y.: Doubleday Anchor Books, 1967), p. 39.

39. In story by George Dugan, *New York Times*, 12 Apr. 1969. About 5,000 Protestant clergymen from every state sponsored a full-page advertisement in the *New York Times* of 18 Nov. 1968, denouncing the World Council of Churches, espousing a right line in domestic and foreign policies, and simultaneously demanding that churches stay out of political and social questions. The ad was explicitly and fanatically anti-Marxist. For an excellent historical study of this conflict, see E. V. Toy, Jr., "The National Lay Committee and the National Council of Churches," *American Quarterly* 21 (Summer 1969): 190–209.

40. Markus Barth, "Churches and Communism in East Germany," *The Christian Century*, 23, 30 Nov. 1966.

41. Roland Warren, as quoted by Jean Edward Smith, "The German Democratic Republic and the West," *Yale Review*, Apr. 1969, p. 373. In 1967, Pope Paul VI named Alfred Bensch of East Berlin a Cardinal, at 42 the youngest Cardinal in German history and the youngest member of the present College of Cardinals.

42. John A. Mackay, "Cuba Revisited," *The Christian Century*, 12 Feb. 1964.

43. Everett Gendler, "Holy Days in Habana," *Conservative Judaism* 23: (Winter 1969): 15–24.

44. Lanternari, *op. cit.*, p. 254.

45. It is worth recalling that the maxim of Reformation ecclesiology was: *ecclesia non solum reformata sed semper reformanda* (a church not only reformed, but ever to be reformed).

46. *World Conference on Church and Society, Geneva, July 12–26. 1966: The Official Report* (Geneva: World Council of Churches, 1967), p. 96, 200, *passim*; Walter M. Abbott, S.J., ed., *The Documents of Vatican II* (New York: Guild Press, 1966), pp. 241n., 243 *passim*.

Chapter 11. Marxism, Religion, and the Future

1. See Curtiss B. Pepper, *An Artist and the Pope* (New York: Grosset & Dunlap, 1968).

2. See Sean Cronin, "The Wearing of the Green," *Commonweal*, 12 July 1968.

3. John Kenneth Galbraith, *The Triumph: A Novel of American Diplomacy* (Boston: Houghton Mifflin Co., 1968).

4. I know, of course, that the basic significance of this is questioned, and that its persistence is denied, but the work of Harry Magdoff, James O' Connor, Dick Roberts, Hyman Lumer, Robert Heilbroner, Gabriel Kolko, Victor Perlo, Herbert Schiller, and the Labor Research Association, among others, is persuasive that such ownership and such purposes of economic activity are fundamental to the American

economic order, the more so as it becomes increasingly monopolistic. Within the limits of this book and its central subject, it is neither practical nor proper to develop such concepts as revolution, or the Marxist approach to democracy, freedom, violence, and so forth. I have tried to do this in *The Nature of Democracy, Freedom and Revolution* (New York: International Publishers, 1967).

5. Harvey Cox, *On Not Leaving It to the Snake* (New York: Macmillan Co., 1967), p. 45.

6. Henri de Lubac, "The New Man: The Marxist and the Christian View," *Dublin Review*, Spring 1948.

7. Marx, *Capital* (New York: International Publishers, 1967), 1:512; see also 1:178, 180, 204, 206, 603–5. For an awareness of the consequence of nature and its conquest as a dynamic in the Marxist concept of history, see E. A. Olssen, "Marx and the Resurrection," *Journal of the History of Ideas* 29 (Jan.-Mar. 1968):136.

8. A. R. Hall, *The Scientific Revolution, 1500–1800* (London, 1954), intro.

9. Robert L. Heilbroner, "The Future of Capitalism," *Quardrant* (Sydney, Australia), Mar.-Apr.1967; reprinted in *Current,* Aug. 1967, p. 53.

10. Lenin, *Collected Works* (Moscow: Foreign Languages Publishing House, 1960), 4:211–12.

11. The Mississippi data are given by TRB in *The New Republic,* 20 July 1968; Gorman's findings are in the *New York Times,* 29 June 1969.

12. Robin Marris, in *American Economic Review,* Mar. 1968, p. 246. The Catholic theologian Bernard Delfgaauw, while noting that establishing socialism means and has meant depriving sections of the population of former rights, continues: ". . . it has also and for the first time made it possible for the great majority of the people to enjoy a fully human mode of living" (*The Young Marx* [London: Sheed& Ward, 1967]), pp. 131–32.

13. *New York Times,* 30 May 1968.

14. *Washington Post,* 4 Feb. 1968.

15. *The Christian Century,* 17 Apr. 1968.

16. James Colaianni, *The Catholic Left* (Philadelphia: Chilton, 1968), p. 28.

17. *New York Times,* 14 May 1968.

18. In R. H. Tawney, *Religion and the Rise of Capitalism* (New York: Harcourt, Brace, 1926), p. 89.

19. Morris R. Cohen, *American Thought: A Critical Sketch* (Glencoe, Ill.: Free Press, 1954), pp. 227–28.

20. James Redpath, *The Public Life of Capt. John Brown* (Boston: Thayer & Eldridge, 1860), p. 382.

21. Walter Rauschenbusch, *Christianity and the Social Crisis,* 10th ed. (New York: Macmillan Co., 1911), pp. 408, 417, 418, 422.

22. Especially important was Kirby Page's *Jesus or Christianity* (New York: Doubleday, Doran, 1929), the October 1929 selection of the Religious Book of the Month Club. A condensed version was published and sold for 15 cents as part of Doubleday, Doran's "Christianity and World Problems" series, which in 10 years (by 1929) had sold over one million copies.

NOTES

23. Harriet Beecher Stowe, *Uncle Tom's Cabin* (Boston, 1852), pp. 507–16.

24. Richard Shaull, "The God Question," *The Christian Century*, 28 Feb. 1968, p. 275.

25. *Commonweal*, 6 Oct. 1967.

26. Eugene C. Bianchi, "Resistance in the Church," *Commonweal*, 16 May 1969, p. 260. See also the quite remarkable essay by Giles Hibbert, a Catholic priest and member of the Dominican Order, "Socialism, Revolution and Christianity," *Labor Monthly* (London), Dec. 1968. He speaks of Christian theologians "who are involved in the dialogue precisely as Socialists, even Marxist Socialists" which "they will claim is fundamental to their Christianity" (p. 560).

27. Roque Dalton, "Catholics and Communists in Latin America," *World Marxist Review*, Jan 1968, pp. 82–90.

28. Gus Hall, *Catholics and Communists: Elements of a Dialogue* (New York: Political Affairs Publishers, 1964), p. 6.

29. C. Wright Mills, *The Marxists* (New York: Dell, 1962), pp. 13–14.